Best Garden Plants *for* Montana

Dr. Bob Gough
Cheryl Moore-Gough
Laura Peters

LONE
PINE

Lone Pine Publishing

Distributed by Lone Pine Publishing
1808 B Street NW, Suite 140
Auburn, WA, USA 98001

Website: www.lonepinepublishing.com

Library and Archives Canada Cataloguing in Publication

Gough, Robert E. (Robert Edward)
    Best garden plants for Montana / Bob Gough, Cheryl Moore-Gough,
Laura Peters.

    Includes index.
    ISBN-13: 978-1-55105-518-3
    ISBN-10: 1-55105-518-X

    1. Plants, Ornamental—Montana. I. Moore-Gough, Cheryl, 1954–
II. Peters, Laura, 1968– III. Title.

SB453.2.M9G69 2005   635.9'09786   C2005-901642-6

Scanning & Digital Film: Elite Lithographers Co.

Front cover photographs by Tamara Eder, except where noted. *Clockwise from top right:* Morden Sunrise (Parkland rose), iris, lilac, daylily 'Dewey Roquemore,' prairie smoke (*Tim Matheson*), Jens Munk (Explorer rose), columbine 'McKana hybrids,' cherry, daylily 'Janet Gayle' (*Allison Penko*)

Photography: All photos by Tamara Eder, Tim Matheson and Laura Peters except:
AAFC 129b; AASelection 31b, 32a; Bailey Nursery Roses 115, 117b; J.C. Bakker & Sons 125a; Brendan Casement 87b; Janet Davis 129a; Joan de Grey 168b; Jen Fafard 144a; Derek Fell 52b, 73, 143a&b, 168a; Erika Flatt 9c, 111b, 141b; Anne Gordon 137b; Jan Hjalmarsson 41a&b, 164a&b; Duncan Kelbaugh 141a; Linda Kershaw 79b; Liz Klose 9a, 113a, 120a, 149a, 151a&b; Dawn Loewen 8c, 77a, 83a, 86a&b; Janet Loughrey 131a&b, 137a; Mark Majerus 162; Marilynn McAra 144b, 145a&b, 146a; Kim O'Leary 24a, 155b; Allison Penko 52a, 58, 64a, 65a, 75a, 87a, 93a, 95a&b, 102a, 103a, 107a&b, 109a, 134a, 167a; Pickering Nurseries 117a; Robert Ritchie 43b, 45a, 114a&b, 123a&b, 124a&b, 126a, 128a&b, 133a, 135a; Joseph Scianna 165; Leila Sidi 64b, 146b; Peter Thompstone 25a, 54a, 56b, 61a, 63a; Mark Turner 71b; USDA-US National Arboretum 82a; Don Williamson 135b, 142a&b.

This book is not intended as a 'how-to' guide for eating garden plants. No plant or plant extract should be consumed unless you are certain of its identity and toxicity and of your potential for allergic reactions.

PC: P1

Table of Contents

Introduction

Starting a garden can seem like a daunting task. Which plants should you choose? Where should you put them in the garden? How should you care for them? This book is intended to give beginning gardeners the information they need to start planning and planting gardens of their own. It describes a wide variety of plants and provides basic planting information such as where and how to plant.

Because of its northern location, Montana has a reputation for extreme and unpredictable weather, but Montanans know that if they wait a minute, the weather will change and often for the better. In fact, Loma, Montana, holds the world record for the greatest temperature change in 24 hours. On January 15, 1972, the temperature rose from –54° F to 49° F—a 103 degree change in 24 hours!

While some residents have less of an appreciation for the dry climate, others revel in it. Low humidity levels occur across the state, resulting in conditions that feel neither overwhelmingly hot nor cold. The weather can vary greatly depending on where you are in the state, however. Average daytime temperatures range from 28° F in January to 85° F in July, but seasonal extremes are more evident on the plains of eastern Montana. Winter temperatures often dip below 0° F, but the cold weather is sometimes offset by Chinook winds (warm, dry winds that blow in from the Rocky Mountains). In western Montana, the winters tend to be milder, the summers cooler and the weather generally wetter.

Snow coverage is relatively reliable, and winter takes its hiatus in April, with small snowfalls persisting into May. Summer is warm and dry, especially in July and August, though nights generally remain cool. Evenings grow colder in September, and the snow makes a triumphant return with scattered flurries here and there, but the real transformation takes place throughout October when the leaves change to fiery shades of orange, yellow and red. Winter snows accumulate in November, and cold weather becomes more consistent. The winter brings dry, fluffy snow that may be several feet deep at upper elevations, remaining well into spring. It's common for the Rocky Mountains to receive up to 25' of snow, but much of Montana remains dry, averaging only 15" of precipitation annually.

Hardiness zones and frost dates are two terms often used when discussing climate. Hardiness zones are based on the temperatures and conditions in winter. Plants are rated based on the zones in which they grow successfully. The last frost date in spring combined with the first frost date in fall allows us to predict the length of the growing season.

Getting Started

When planning your garden, start with a quick analysis of the garden as it is now. Plants have different requirements, and it is best to put the right plant in the right place rather than to try to change your garden to suit the plants you want.

Knowing which parts of your garden receive the most and least amounts of sunlight will help you choose the proper plants and decide where to plant them. Light is classified into four basic levels: full sun (direct, unobstructed light all or most of the day); partial shade (direct sun for about half the day and shade for

the rest); light shade (shade all or most of the day with some sun filtering through to ground level); and full shade (no direct sunlight). Most plants prefer a certain amount of light but many can adapt to a range of light levels.

Plants use the soil to hold themselves upright, but they also rely on the many resources it holds: air, water, nutrients, organic matter and a host of microbes. The particle size of the soil influences the amount of air, water and nutrients it can hold. Sand, with the largest particles, has a lot of air space and allows water and

Average Annual Minimum Temperature

Zone	Temp (°F)
2b	−40 to −45
3a	−35 to −40
3b	−30 to −35
4a	−25 to −30
4b	−20 to −25
5a	−15 to −20
5b	−10 to −15
6a	−5 to −10

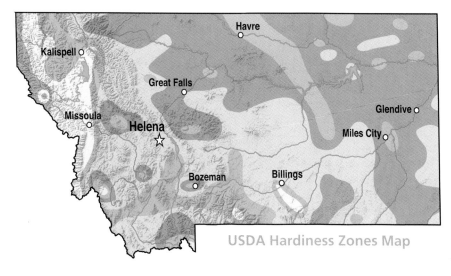

USDA Hardiness Zones Map

nutrients to drain quickly. Clay, with the smallest particles, is high in nutrients but has very little air space. Water is therefore slow to penetrate clay and slow to drain from it.

Soil acidity or alkalinity (measured on the pH scale) influences the nutrients available to plants. A pH of 7 is neutral; a lower pH is more acidic. Most plants prefer a soil with a pH of 5.5–7.5. Soil-testing kits are available at most garden centers, and soil samples can be sent to testing facilities for a more thorough analysis.

Compost is one of the best and most important amendments you can add to any type of soil. Compost improves soil by adding organic matter and nutrients, introducing soil microbes, increasing water retention and improving drainage. Compost can be purchased or you can make it in your own backyard.

Microclimates are small areas that are generally warmer or colder than the surrounding area. Buildings, fences, trees and other large structures can provide extra shelter in winter but may trap heat in summer, thus creating a warmer microclimate. The bottoms of hills are usually colder than the tops but may not be as windy. Take advantage of these areas when you plan your garden and choose your plants; you may even grow out-of-zone plants successfully in a warm, sheltered location. For example, mountain ash will generally perform better in a sheltered location than in an exposed spot.

Selecting Plants

It's important to purchase healthy plants that are free of pests and diseases. Such plants will establish quickly in your garden and won't introduce problems that may spread to other plants. You should have a good idea of what the plant is supposed to look like—its habit, and the color and shape of its leaves—and then inspect the plant for signs of disease or infestation.

The majority of plants in nurseries and greenhouses are container grown. This is an efficient way to grow plants, but when plants grow in a restricted space for too long, they can become pot bound, their roots densely encircling the inside of the pot. Avoid purchasing plants in this condition because they are often stressed and can take longer to establish. In some cases, they may not establish at all. It is often possible to remove pots temporarily to look at the condition of the roots. You can check for soil-borne insects and rotten roots at the same time.

Planting Basics

The following tips apply to all plants.
• Prepare the garden before planting. Dig over the soil, pull up any weeds and make any needed amendments before you begin planting, if possible. This may be more difficult in established beds to which you want to add a single plant.

1. Gently remove container.

2. Ensure proper planting depth.

3. Backfill with soil.

The prepared area should be at least twice the size of the plant you want to put in, and preferably the expected size of the mature plant.

• Unwrap the roots. It is always best to remove any container before planting to give roots the chance to spread out naturally when planted. In particular, you should remove plastic containers, fiber pots, wire and anything posing as "burlap" before planting trees. Fiber pots decompose very slowly, if at all, and wick moisture away from the plant, and wire can eventually strangle the roots as they mature. The only exceptions to this rule are peat pots and pellets used to start annuals and vegetables; these decompose and can be planted with the young transplants. Use a knife to slice the mesh surrounding the peat pellets, for better root distribution.

• Accommodate the rootball. If you prepared your planting spot ahead of time, your planting hole will only need to be big enough to accommodate the rootball with the roots spread out slightly.

• Know the mature size of the plant. Plant based on how big the plants will grow rather than how big they are when you plant them. Large plants should have enough room to mature without interfering with walls, roof overhangs, power lines and walkways.

• Plant at the same depth. Plants generally like to grow at a certain level in relation to the soil and should be planted at the same level they were before you transplanted them.

• Settle the soil with water. Good contact between the roots and the soil is important, but if you press the soil down too firmly, as often happens when you step on the soil, you can cause compaction. Compaction reduces the movement of water through the soil and leaves very few air spaces. Instead, pour water in as you fill the hole with soil. The water will settle the soil evenly without allowing it to compact.

• Identify your plants. Keep track of what's what in your garden by putting a tag next to your plant when you plant it. It is very easy for beginning gardeners to forget exactly what they planted and where they planted it. Although we always tag new transplants, each spring we get a surprise. Either something comes back that we forgot we planted, or we just can't identify the dead brown stubs that evidently did not survive the winter. Remove wire or plastic tags from woody nursery stock to prevent stem girdling.

• Water deeply and infrequently. It's better to water deeply once every week or two rather than water superficially several times a week. Less frequent watering forces roots to grow to search for water and helps them survive dry spells when water bans may restrict your watering regime. Always check the rootzone

4. Settle backfilled soil with water.

5. Water the plant well.

6. Add a layer of mulch.

before you water to make sure the soil is actually dry. More gardeners overwater than underwater.

Annuals

Annuals are planted new each year and are only expected to last for a single growing season. Their flowers and decorative foliage provide bright splashes of color and can fill in spaces around immature trees, shrubs and perennials.

Calendula

Annuals are easy to plant and are usually sold in small packs of four or six. The roots quickly fill the space in these small packs, so the small rootball should be broken up before planting. You can often break the ball in two up the center or run your thumb up each side to break up the roots.

Some annuals are grown from seed and can be started directly in the garden.

Perennials

Perennials grow for three or more years. They usually die back to the ground each fall and send up new shoots in spring, though some are evergreen. They often

Prairie coneflower

have a shorter period of bloom than annuals but require less care.

Many perennials benefit from being divided every few years. This keeps them growing and blooming vigorously, and in some cases controls their spread. Dividing involves digging the plant up, removing dead bits, breaking the plant into several pieces and replanting some or all of the pieces. Extra pieces can be given as gifts to family, friends and neighbors. Consult a perennial book for further information on the care of perennials.

Trees & Shrubs

Trees and shrubs provide the bones of the garden. They are often the slowest growing plants but usually live the longest. Characterized by leaf type, they may be deciduous or evergreen, and needled or broad-leaved.

Arborvitae

Trees should have as little disturbed soil as possible at the bottom of the planting hole. Loose soil settles over time and sinking even an inch can kill some trees.

Staking, sometimes recommended for newly planted trees, is only necessary for trees over 5' tall or trees planted in windy locations. Allow stakes to remain in place for no more than one year.

Pruning is more often required for shrubs than for trees. It helps them maintain an attractive shape and can improve blooming. Consult a book on pruning or take a pruning course for information about pruning trees and shrubs.

Roses

Roses are beautiful shrubs with lovely, often fragrant, blooms. Traditionally, most roses only bloomed once in the growing season, but currently available varieties often bloom more than once during the warm summer months.

Clematis

John Cabot

Generally, roses prefer a fertile, well-prepared planting area. A rule of thumb is to prepare an area 24" across, front to back and side to side, and 24" deep. Add plenty of compost or other fertile organic matter and keep roses well watered during the growing season. Many roses are quite durable and will adapt to poorer conditions.

Roses, like all shrubs, have specific pruning requirements. Consult a reputable rose book for more detailed information.

Vines

Vines or climbing plants are useful for screening and shade, especially in a location too small for a tree. They may be woody or herbaceous and annual or perennial.

Most vines need sturdy supports to grow on. Trellises, arbors, porch railings, fences, walls, poles and trees are all possible supports. If a support is needed,

ensure it's in place before you plant to avoid disturbing the roots later.

Bulbs, Corms, Tubers

These plants have fleshy underground storage organs that allow them to survive extended periods of dormancy. They are often grown for the bright splashes of color their flowers provide. They may be spring, summer or fall flowering.

Crocus

Hardy bulbs can be left in the ground and will flower every year, but many popular tender plants grow from bulbs, corms or tubers. These tender plants are generally lifted from the garden in fall as the foliage dies back, and are stored in a cool, frost-free location for winter, to be replanted in spring.

Herbs

Herbs may be medicinal or culinary and are often both. A few common culinary herbs are listed in this book. Even if you don't cook with herbs, the often-fragrant foliage adds its aroma to the garden and the plants can be quite decorative in form, leaf and flower.

Basil

Many herbs have pollen-producing flowers that attract butterflies, bees and hummingbirds to your garden. They also attract predatory insects. These useful insects help to manage your pest problems by feasting on problem insects such as aphids, mealybugs and whiteflies.

Ornamental Grasses and Other Foliage Plants

Foliage is an important consideration when choosing plants for your garden. Although many plants look spectacular in bloom, they can seem rather dull without flowers. Including a variety of plants with unique, interesting or striking foliage in your garden can provide all the color and texture you want without the need to rely on flowers.

Ornamental grasses are becoming very popular additions to the garden. Grasses offer a variety of textures and foliage colors, and at least three seasons

Artemisia

of interest. There is an ornamental grass for every garden situation and condition. Some grasses will thrive in any garden condition, including hot and dry to cool and wet, and in all types of soils. Ornamental grasses have very few insect or disease problems. They require very little maintenance other than cutting the perennial grasses back in fall or spring.

We have included some grass-like foliage plants in this book, and they can be used with or as a substitute for ornamental grasses. We have also added a variety of plants grown for their foliage throughout the book. Many annuals, perennials, trees, shrubs, vines and herbs have wonderful foliage, and they will be an asset to your garden landscape.

A Final Comment

Don't be afraid to experiment. No matter how many books you read, trying things yourself is the best way to learn and to find out what will grow in your garden. Use the information provided as guidelines, and have fun!

Ageratum
Ageratum

Ageratum is an amazing butterfly magnet. It offers a constant supply of nectar to many butterfly species throughout summer and fall.

Growing
Ageratum flowers best in **full sun** but tolerates partial shade. The soil should be **fertile, moist** and **well drained**. This plant doesn't like to have its soil dry out; a moisture-retaining mulch will reduce the need for water.

Tips
The smaller varieties, which are often completely covered with fluffy flowerheads, make excellent edging plants for flowerbeds and pathways. They are also attractive grouped in masses or grown in planters. The taller varieties work well in the center of a flowerbed or interplanted with other annuals They also make interesting cut flowers.

Recommended
A. houstonianum has clusters of fuzzy blue, white or pink flowers and forms a large, leggy mound that can grow up to 24" tall. Many cultivars are available; most, including the **Danube** and **Hawaii Series**, have a low, compact form that makes them popular choices for border plantings. Others, such as the **Horizon Series** and **'Leilani,'** are much taller and make good cut flowers.

A. houstonianum (above & below)

Although this plant requires deadheading to keep it flowering, the blossoms are extraordinarily long-lived.

Also called: floss flower **Features:** flowers; habit **Flower color:** white, pink, mauve, blue, purple **Height**: 6–36" **Spread:** 6–18"

Annual Delphinium

Consolida

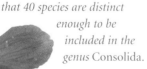

C. ambigua (above & below)

C. ambigua was once treated as an annual species of delphinium (Delphinium), but botanists now agree that 40 species are distinct enough to be included in the genus Consolida.

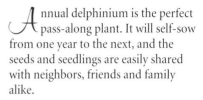

*A*nnual delphinium is the perfect pass-along plant. It will self-sow from one year to the next, and the seeds and seedlings are easily shared with neighbors, friends and family alike.

Growing

Annual delphinium does equally well in **full sun** or **light shade**. The soil should be **fertile, rich in organic matter** and **well drained**. Keep the roots cool and add a light mulch; dried grass clippings or shredded leaves work well. Don't put mulch too close to the base of the plant, or crown rot may develop. Another option is to plant annual delphinium close together so that the centers of plants are only 6–8" apart. The upper portion of the plants will then shade the roots, so you will not need to use mulch.

Tips

Plant groups of annual delphinium in mixed borders, cutting beds or cottage gardens. The tallest varieties may require staking to stay upright.

Recommended

C. ambigua (*C. ajacis; Delphinium ajacis*) is an upright plant with feathery foliage and tall flower spikes. **Dwarf Rocket Series** includes plants that grow 12–20" tall and 6–10" wide and bloom in many colors. **Giant Imperial Series** has plants that grow 24–36" tall and up to 14" wide and come in many colors.

Also called: rocket larkspur, larkspur
Features: attractive flowers **Flower color:** blue, purple, pink, white **Height:** 12"–4'
Spread: 6–14"

Bachelor's Buttons
Centaurea

C. cyanus (above & below)

Bachelor's buttons is an old-time favorite, and it continues to be a popular and highly desirable annual today.

Growing
Bachelor's buttons grows best in **full sun. Average to fertile, moist, well-drained** soil is preferable, but it tolerates any soil, including poor and dry soil. Light frost won't harm this plant.

Seeds started indoors should be planted in peat pots or pellets to avoid disturbing roots during transplanting. Plant out around the last frost. Shear spent flowers and old foliage in mid-summer for fresh new growth. Deadheading will prolong blooming.

Tips
Bachelor's buttons is useful in a mixed border, wildflower bed or cottage-style garden. It looks great when massed, works well in containers and makes a wonderful cut flower.

Recommended
C. cyanus is an upright annual that self-seeds year after year. Many cultivars are available.

In a garden with poor, rocky or sandy soil, pair this tough, hard-to-kill plant with California poppies for a bright, summer display.

Also called: cornflower **Features:** bright flowers; tough, self-seeding plant **Flower color:** mostly blue, with shades of red, pink, white, purple **Height:** 8–32" **Spread:** 6–24"

Calendula

Calendula

'Apricot Surprise' (above); *C. officinalis* (below)

Calendulas are bright and charming, producing attractive flowers in warm colors all summer and fall.

Growing

Calendula does equally well in **full sun** or **partial shade**. It likes cool weather and can withstand a moderate frost. The soil should be of **average fertility** and **well drained**. Deadhead to prolong blooming and keep plants looking neat. If plants fade in summer heat, cut them back to 4–6" above the ground to promote new growth, or pull them up and seed new ones. Either method will provide a good fall display. Sow seed directly into the garden in mid-spring, especially in eastern Montana because of the short season.

Tips

This informal plant looks attractive in borders or mixed into the vegetable patch. It can also be used in mixed planters. Calendula is a cold-hardy annual and often continues flowering, even through a layer of snow, until the ground freezes completely.

Recommended

C. officinalis is a vigorous, tough, upright plant that bears daisy-like, single or double flowers in a wide range of yellow and orange shades. Several cultivars are available.

Also called: pot marigold, English marigold
Features: colorful flowers; long blooming period **Flower color:** cream, yellow, gold, orange, apricot **Height:** 10–24" **Spread:** 8–20"

California Poppy

Eschscholzia

California poppies cheerfully reseed themselves year after year. They look great in meadow or rock gardens, or popping up through the cracks of a flagstone path.

Growing

California poppy prefers **full sun** and **well-drained** soil of **poor to average fertility**. In rich soil, the plant will grow lush and green, but will bear few, if any, flowers. This plant is drought tolerant once established, but it requires a lot of water for germination and until it begins to flower.

Never start this plant indoors because it dislikes having its roots disturbed. California poppy will sprout quickly when sown directly in the garden in early to mid-spring. In mild areas, seeds sown in early fall will produce blooms in spring.

Tips

California poppy can be included in an annual border or annual planting in a cottage garden.

Recommended

E. californica forms a mound of delicate, feathery, blue-green foliage. It bears satiny flowers all summer. Cultivars with semi-double or double flowers and flowers in red, cream or pink are available.

E. californica (above & below)

The petals of California poppy can be eaten. They have little nutritional value but the color will brighten up a salad.

Features: colorful flowers; attractive, feathery foliage **Flower color:** orange, yellow, red; less commonly pink, violet or cream **Height:** 12–24" **Spread:** 6–12"

Candytuft

Iberis

I. umbellata (above & below)

Candytuft is invaluable for bringing soft, soothing color to semi-shady portions of the yard and garden.

Growing
Candytuft prefers to grow in **full sun** or **partial shade**. Partial shade is best if it gets very hot in your garden. Like many species in the mustard family, candytuft dislikes heat; blooming will often slow down or decrease in July and August. The soil should be of **poor** or **average fertility**, **well drained** and have a neutral or alkaline pH.

Deadheading when the seeds begin to form will keep candytuft blooming, but do let some plants go to seed to guarantee repeat performances.

Tips
This informal plant can be used on rock walls, in mixed containers or as edging for beds.

Recommended
I. umbellata produces dense, rounded flower heads that emerge in late spring through summer. This upright, bushy plant bears mid-green, lance-shaped foliage on short stems. **Dwarf Fairy Series** ('Dwarf Fairyland') plants are compact and bear many flowers in a variety of pastel shades.

Candytuft is a frost-hardy plant in most regions and is often used as a cut flower.

Also called: globe candytuft **Features:** profuse flowering habit **Flower color:** white, pink, purple, red **Height:** 6–12" **Spread:** 8" or more

China Aster
Callistephus

China aster's vivid and dense flowers will steal the spotlight in your garden all summer long.

Growing
China aster prefers **full sun** but tolerates partial shade. The soil should be **fertile, evenly moist** and **well drained**. A **neutral** or **alkaline** pH is preferable. If your garden has acidic soil, grow smaller China aster varieties in pots or planters, where the soil pH can be more easily adjusted.

Plant out once the soil has warmed. This plant doesn't like having its roots disturbed, so start seeds in peat pots or peat pellets. China aster has a shallow root system that can dry out quickly; mulch to conserve moisture.

Tips
Use smaller varieties as edging plants and taller varieties for cut flowers and at the back of the border. Tall varieties may require staking.

Recommended
C. chinensis is the source of many varieties and cultivars, which come in three height groups: dwarf, medium and tall. '**Comet**' is an early-flowering cultivar of medium height, bearing large, quilled, double flowers. '**Duchess**' plants are wilt resistant. Tall, sturdy stems bear colorful flowers with petals that curve in towards the center. '**Meteor**' are tall plants with large, yellow-centered flowers. '**Pot 'n' Patio**' is a popular dwarf cultivar with double flowers, and '**Princess**' is of medium height with quilled, double or semi-double flowers in a wide range of colors.

C. chinensis cultivars (above & below)

China asters are heavy feeders, so you will need to fertilize them regularly to produce flowers like those seen in catalogs.

Features: colorful flowers of varying shapes and sizes **Flower color:** purple, blue, pink, red, white, peach, yellow **Height:** 12–36" **Spread:** 10–18"

Clarkia
Clarkia

C. amoena (above); C. amoena cultivar (below)

These plants don't like to be overwatered, so water sparingly and be sure to let them dry out between waterings. They do best in the cool weather of spring and fall.

Starting seeds indoors is not recommended. Seed plants where you want them to grow because they are difficult to transplant. Thin seedlings to about 6" apart.

Tips
Clarkia are useful in beds, borders, containers and rock gardens. The flowers can be used in fresh arrangements. These plants flower quickly from seed and can be planted in early spring to provide a show of satiny flowers before the hardier summer annuals steal the show.

A planting in mid-summer will provide flowers in fall.

Recommended
C. amoena (*Godetia amoena; G. grandiflora*) is a bushy, upright plant, bearing clusters of ruffled, cup-shaped flowers. **Satin Series** is more compact, with single flowers in varied solid and bicolored combinations.

C. unguiculata (*C. elegans*; clarkia, Rocky Mountain garland flower) is a tall, branching plant with small, ruffled flowers in pink, purple, red or white. **'Apple Blossom'** bears double, apricot pink flowers. **'Royal Bouquet'** bears very ruffled, double flowers in pink, red or light purple.

ighly valued by the floral industry, the delicate, papery flowers of clarkia are equally appreciated by gardeners for their lasting vase quality and sheer beauty.

Growing
Clarkia grows equally well in **full sun** or **light shade**. The soil should be **well drained, light, sandy** and of **poor or average fertility**. Fertilizer will promote leaf growth at the expense of flower production.

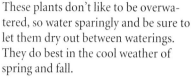

Also called: godetia, satin flower **Features:** delicate, colorful flowers; habit **Flower color:** pink, red, purple, white, some bicolored **Height:** 8"–4' **Spread:** 10–12"

Cleome
Cleome

C. hassleriana (above & below)

Create a bold and exotic display in your garden with these lovely and unusual flowers.

Growing

Cleome prefers **full sun** but tolerates **partial shade**. Plants **adapt to most soils**, though mixing in organic matter to help retain water is a good idea. These plants are drought tolerant but perform best when watered regularly. Pinch out the tip of the center stem on young plants to encourage branching and more blooms. Deadhead to prolong blooming and reduce prolific self-seeding.

Tips

Cleome can be planted in groups at the back or a border or in the center of an island bed. These striking plants also make an attractive addition to a large mixed container planting.

Recommended

C. hassleriana is a tall, upright plant with strong, supple, thorny stems. The foliage and flowers of this plant have a strong but not unpleasant scent. Flowers are borne in loose, rounded clusters at the ends of the leafy stems. Many cultivars are available.

C. serrulata (Rocky Mountain bee plant) is native to western North America, but it is rarely available commercially. The thornless, dwarf cultivar **'Solo'** is regularly available to be grown from seed and grows 12–18" tall with pink and white flowers.

Also called: spider flower **Features:** attractive, scented foliage and flowers; thorny stems **Flower color:** purple, pink, white **Height:** 12"–5' **Spread:** 12–24"

Cosmos
Cosmos

C. bipinnatus (above); C. bipinnatus cultivar (below)

Look for C. atrosanguineus *(chocolate cosmos); on a hot day, it smells like chocolate.*

C osmos flowers are deeply saturated with color and provide nectar for various butterflies. The fluted petals of cosmos add an interesting texture to the garden and the flower vase.

Growing
Cosmos likes **full sun**. The soil should be of **poor or average fertility** and **well drained**. Cosmos is drought tolerant. Overfertilizing and overwatering can reduce the number of flowers produced. Keep faded blooms cut to encourage more buds. Often, this plant reseeds itself.

Tips
Cosmos is attractive planted in cottage gardens, at the back of a border, or en masse in an informal bed or border. Taller varieties will likely need staking.

Recommended
C. bipinnatus (annual cosmos) has many cultivars. The flowers come in a variety of colors, usually with yellow centers. Old varieties grow tall, while some of the newer cultivars remain quite short. **Sea Shells Series** has flowers in all colors and petals that are rolled into tubes.

Features: colorful flowers; fern-like foliage
Flower color: white, yellow, gold, orange, shades of pink and red **Height:** 12"–6'
Spread: 12–18"

Dusty Miller

Senecio

S. cineraria 'Cirrus' (above); S. cineraria (below)

Dusty miller makes an artful addition to planters, window boxes and mixed borders where the soft, silvery gray, deeply-lobed foliage makes a good backdrop to show off the brightly colored flowers of other annuals.

Growing

Dusty miller prefers **full sun** but tolerates light shade. The soil should be of **average fertility** and **well drained**.

Tips

The soft, silvery, lacy leaves of this plant are its main feature. Dusty miller is used primarily as an edging plant, but also in beds, borders and containers.

Pinch off the flowers before they bloom. They aren't showy, and they steal energy that would otherwise go to producing more foliage.

Recommended

S. cineraria forms a mound of fuzzy, silvery gray, lobed or finely divided foliage. Many cultivars have been developed with impressive foliage colors and shapes.

Mix dusty miller with geraniums, begonias or cockscombs (Celosia) to bring out the vibrant colors of those flowers.

Features: silvery foliage; neat habit **Flower color:** yellow to cream; grown for silvery foliage **Height:** 12–24" **Spread:** equal to height or slightly narrower

Four-O'Clock Flower

Mirabilis

M. jalapa cultivars (above & below)

An old-fashioned favorite, four-o'clock flower has been grown for generations and is often included in the heritage gardens of today.

Growing

Four-o'clock flower prefers **full sun** but tolerates partial shade. The soil should be **fertile**, though any **well-drained** soil is tolerated. This plant grows well in moist soil, but it is heat and drought tolerant.

Four-o'clock flower is a perennial treated as an annual, and it may be grown from tuberous roots. Dig up the roots in fall, store them in a cool, dry place and replant them in spring to enjoy larger plants.

All parts of four-o'clock flower are poisonous, including the large black seeds. With the current trend of eating flowers, it is important that this plant be on the 'do not eat' list.

Tips

Four-o'clock flower can be used in beds, borders, containers and window boxes. The flowers are scented, so the plant is often located near deck patios or terraces where the scent can be enjoyed in the afternoon and evening.

Recommended

M. jalapa forms a bushy mound of foliage. The flowers may be solid or bicolored, and a single plant may bear flowers of several colors. 'Marvel of Peru,' listed as a common name or as a cultivar name, features the multi-colored flowers four-o'clock flower is known for. 'Red Glow' bears brilliant red flowers. 'Tea Time' bears a single flower color on each plant. Flowers may be red, white or pink.

Features: flowers; habit **Flower color:** red, pink, magenta, yellow, white, bicolored
Height: 18–36" **Spread:** 18–24"

Gaillardia
Gaillardia

This native annual is sure to turn up the heat in your garden with its fiery shades of yellow, red, orange and every shade and combination in between.

Growing
Gaillardia prefers **full sun**. The soil should be of **poor** or **average fertility, light, sandy** and **well drained**. The less water this plant receives, the better it will do. Don't cover the seeds; they need light to germinate. They also require warm soil.

Deadhead to encourage more blooms.

Tips
Gaillardia has an informal, sprawling habit that makes it a perfect addition to a casual cottage garden or mixed border. Because it is drought tolerant, gaillardia is well suited to exposed, sunny slopes, where it can help retain soil while more permanent plants grow in.

G. *pulchella* (above & below)

Make sure to place this flower in a location where it will not get watered with other plants.

Almost every species from this genus of annuals, perennials and biennials is native to the U.S.

Recommended
G. pulchella forms a basal rosette of leaves. The daisy-like flowers are red with yellow tips. **Plume Series** plants produce double flowerheads in vibrant shades of red or yellow.

Features: brightly colored, long-lasting flowers; habit **Flower color:** red, orange, yellow, often in combination **Height:** 12–36" **Spread:** 12–24"

Globe Amaranth
Gomphrena

G. globosa with nasturtiums (above); G. globosa (below)

The clover-like heads actually consist of showy bracts (modified leaves) from which the tiny flowers emerge.

This annual is an everlasting favorite with gardeners and crafters alike for its long-lasting, fade-resistant flowers, both fresh and dried.

Growing
Globe amaranth prefers **full sun**. The soil should be of **average fertility** and **well drained**. This plant likes hot weather. It needs watering only when drought-like conditions persist. Seeds will germinate more quickly if soaked in water for two to four days before sowing. They need warm soil, above 70° F, to sprout.

The long-lasting flowers require only occasional deadheading.

Tips
Use globe amaranth in an informal or cottage garden. This plant is often underused because it doesn't start flowering until later in summer. However, don't overlook globe amaranth—the blooms are worth the wait and provide color from mid-summer until the first frost.

Recommended
G. globosa forms a rounded, bushy plant that is dotted with papery, clover-like flowers. **Buddy Series** offers compact plants, while **'Lavender Lady'** grows into a large plant that bears lavender purple flowers. **'Strawberry Fields'** has bright orange-red or red flowers.

Features: great, everlasting blooms; form **Flower color:** purple, orange, magenta, pink, white, sometimes red **Height:** 6–30"
Spread: 6–15"

Impatiens
Impatiens

*I*mpatiens are the high-wattage darlings of the shade garden, delivering masses of flowers in a wide variety of colors.

Growing

Impatiens do best in **partial shade** or **light shade** but tolerate full shade or, if kept moist, full sun. New Guinea impatiens are the best adapted to sunny locations. The soil should be **fertile, humus rich, moist** and **well drained**.

Tips

Impatiens are known for their ability to grow and flower profusely, even in shade. Mass plant them in beds under trees, along shady fences or walls, or in porch planters. They also look lovely in hanging baskets. New Guinea impatiens are grown as much for their variegated leaves as for their flowers.

Recommended

I. hawkeri (New Guinea hybrids, New Guinea impatiens) flowers in shades of red, orange, pink, purple or white. The foliage is often variegated, with a yellow stripe down the center of each leaf.

I. wallerana (impatiens, busy Lizzie) flowers in shades of purple, red, burgundy, pink, yellow, salmon, orange, apricot, white and can be bicolored. Dozens of cultivars are available.

I. hawkeri (above & below)

The English named I. wallerana *busy Lizzie because it flowers continuously through the growing season.*

Also called: busy Lizzie **Features:** colorful flowers; grows well in shade **Flower color:** purple, red, burgundy, pink, yellow, salmon, orange, apricot, white, bicolored **Height:** 6–36" **Spread:** 12–24"

Lobelia

Lobelia

Lobelia is a lovely plant that adds color to shady spots and blends well with fuchsias and begonias. Lobelia also does well in the sun. Lobelias and marigolds make a striking combination.

Growing

Lobelia grows well in **full sun** or **partial shade** in **fertile, moist, well-drained** soil high in **organic matter**. Lobelia likes cool summer nights. Ensure that its soil stays moist in hot weather. Plant out after the last frost.

Because seedlings are prone to damping off, be sure to use good, clean, seed-starting soil mix. Damping off causes plants to rot at the soil level, flop over and die.

Tips

Use lobelia along the edges of beds and borders, on rock walls, in rock gardens, mixed containers and hanging baskets.

Trim lobelia back after its first wave of flowers. This helps ensure the plant flowers through summer. In hot areas, it may die back over summer but usually revives as the weather cools.

Recommended

L. erinus may be rounded and bushy, or low and trailing, Many cultivars are available in both forms.

L. erinus Cascade Series (above); *L. erinus* cultivar (below)

These lovely plants from the bellflower family contain deadly alkaloids and have poisoned people who tried to use them as herbal medicine.

Features: abundant, colorful flowers **Flower color:** purple, blue, pink, white, red **Height:** 3–9" **Spread:** 6" or more

Love-in-a-Mist

Nigella

N. damascena (above & below)

Love-in-a-mist's ferny foliage and delicate, blue flowers blend beautifully with most plants. It has a tendency to self-sow and may show up in unexpected spots in your garden for years to come.

Growing
Love-in-a-mist prefers **full sun**. The soil should be of **average fertility, light** and **well drained**.

In eastern Montana, the spring season is a long one, so direct sow seeds at two-week intervals all spring to prolong the blooming period. These plants will self-seed, but they resent being disturbed. Seedlings should be transplanted carefully, if at all.

Tips
This attractive, airy plant is often used in mixed beds and borders. The unusual

flowers appear to float above the delicate foliage. Blooming may be slow and the plants may die back if the weather gets too hot in summer. Cut plants back to rejuvenate them.

The stems of this plant can be a bit floppy and may benefit from being staked with twiggy branches. Poke the branches into the soil around the plant when it is young, and the plant will grow up between the twigs.

Recommended
N. damascena forms a loose mound of finely divided foliage. Cultivars are available in a variety of flower colors and forms, including bicolored and double flowers.

The aromatic seeds of love-in-a-mist have been used as a cooking spice and for medicinal purposes.

Also called: devil-in-a-bush **Features:** feathery foliage; exotic flowers; interesting seedpods **Flower color:** blue, white, pink, purple **Height:** 16–24" **Spread:** 8–12"

Marigold

Tagetes

T. tenuifolia (above); *T. patula* cultivar (below)

From the large, exotic, ruffled flowers of African marigold to the tiny flowers on the low-growing signet marigold, the warm colors and fresh scent of marigolds add a festive touch to the garden.

Growing

Marigolds grow best in **full sun**. The soil should be of **average fertility** and **well drained**. These plants are drought tolerant and hold up well in windy, rainy weather. Sow seed directly in the garden after the chance of frost has passed. Deadhead to prolong blooming and to keep plants tidy.

Tips

Mass planted or mixed with other plants, marigolds make a vibrant addition to beds, borders and container gardens. These plants will thrive in the hottest, driest parts of your garden.

Recommended

Many cultivars are available. *T. erecta* (African marigold, American marigold, Aztec marigold) has the largest plants with the biggest flowers; *T. patula* (French marigold) is low growing and comes in a wide range of flower colors; *T. tenuifolia* (signet marigold) has become more popular recently because of its feathery foliage and small, dainty flowers; *T.* **Triploid Hybrids** (triploid marigold), developed by crossing French and African marigolds, have huge flowers and compact growth.

Features: brightly colored flowers; fragrant foliage **Flower color:** yellow, red, orange, brown, gold, cream, bicolored **Height:** 6–36" **Spread:** 12–24"

Moss Rose

Portulaca

$\mathcal{F}$or a brilliant show in the hottest, driest, most sun-baked and neglected area of the garden, you can't go wrong with moss rose.

Growing

Moss rose requires **full sun**. The soil should be of **poor fertility, sandy** and **well drained**. To ensure that you have plants where you want them, start seeds indoors. If you sow directly outdoors, the tiny seeds may get washed away by rain, and the seedlings will pop up in unexpected places. This often occurs, but new plants can be transplanted as needed.

Tips

Moss rose is the ideal flower for garden spots that just don't get enough water, such as under the eaves of a house or in dry, rocky, exposed areas along pathways and in rock walls. It is also an ideal plant for people who like baskets hung from a sunny porch but sometimes neglect to water.

Recommended

P. grandiflora forms a bushy mound of succulent foliage. It bears delicate, silky, rose-like, single or double flowers profusely all summer. Many cultivars are available, including those with flowers that stay open on cloudy days.

P. grandiflora (above & below)

Place these plants close together and allow them to intertwine for an interesting and attractive effect.

Also called: purslane **Features:** colorful, drought- and heat-resistant flowers **Flower color:** red, pink, yellow, white, purple, orange, peach **Height:** 4–8" **Spread:** 6–12" or more

Nasturtium

Tropaeolum

T. majus Alaska Mixed (above & below)

The leaves and flowers of nasturtium are edible, adding a peppery flavor to salads.

These fast-growing, brightly colored flowers are easy to grow, making them popular with beginners and experienced gardeners alike.

Growing

Nasturtiums prefer **full sun** but tolerate some shade. The soil should be of **poor to average fertility, light, moist** and **well drained**. Soil that is too rich or has too much nitrogen fertilizer will result in a lot of leaves and very few flowers. Let the soil drain completely between waterings. Sow directly in the garden once the danger of frost has passed.

Tips

Nasturtiums are used in beds, borders, containers and hanging baskets and on sloped banks. The climbing varieties are grown up trellises or over rock walls or places that need concealing. These plants thrive in poor locations, and they make an interesting addition to plantings on hard-to-mow slopes.

Recommended

T. majus has a trailing habit, but many of the cultivars have bushier, more refined habits. Cultivars offer differing flower colors or variegated foliage.

Features: brightly colored, edible flowers; attractive, edible leaves; varied habits **Flower color:** red, orange, yellow, burgundy, pink, cream, gold, white, bicolored **Height:** 12–18" for dwarf varieties; up to 10' for trailing varieties **Spread:** equal to height

Pansy
Viola

Pansies are one of the most popular annuals available, and for good reason. They're often planted in early spring, long before any other annual, because they tolerate frost like no other. They continue to bloom and bloom and require little care.

Growing
Pansies prefer **full sun** but tolerate partial shade. The soil should be **fertile, moist** and **well drained**. Pansies do best in cool weather.

Tips
Pansies can be used in beds and borders or mixed with spring-flowering bulbs. They can also be grown in containers. With the varied color combinations available, pansies complement almost every other type of bedding plant.

Plant a second crop of pansies late in summer to refresh tired flowerbeds well into the cool months of fall.

Recommended
V. x *wittrockiana* is available in a wide variety of solid, patterned, bicolored and multi-colored flowers with face-like markings in every size imaginable. The foliage is bright green and lightly scalloped along the edges.

V. x *wittrockiana* cultivar (above); 'Ultima Morpho' (below)

The more you pick, the more profusely the plants will bloom, so deadhead throughout the summer months.

Also called: viola **Features:** colorful flowers **Flower color:** blue, purple, red, orange, yellow, pink, white, multi-colored **Height:** 3–10" **Spread:** 6–12"

Petunia
Petunia

'Tidal Wave Silver' (above); multiflora type (below)

The name petunia *is derived from* petun, *the Brazilian word for tobacco, which comes from the species of the related genus* Nicotiana.

For speedy growth, prolific blooming and ease of care, petunias are hard to beat.

Growing
Petunias prefer **full sun**. The soil should be of **average to rich fertility, light, sandy** and **well drained**. Pinch halfway back in mid-summer to keep plants bushy and to encourage new growth and flowers.

Tips
Use petunias in beds, borders, containers and hanging baskets.

Recommended
P. x *hybrida* is a large group of popular, sun-loving annuals that fall into three categories: **grandifloras** have the largest flowers in the widest range of colors, but they can be damaged by rain; **multifloras** bear more flowers that are smaller and less easily damaged by heavy rain; and the **millifloras** have the smallest flowers in the narrowest range of colors, but this type is the most prolific and least likely to be damaged by heavy rain.

Features: colorful flowers; versatility **Flower color:** pink, purple, red, white, yellow, coral, blue, bicolored **Height:** 6–18" **Spread:** 12–24" or more

Poppy
Papaver

*P*oppies look like they were meant to grow in groups. Swaying in a breeze on often-curving stems, the flowers seem engaged in lively conversation.

Growing
Poppies grow best in **full sun**. The soil should be **fertile** and **sandy** with a lot of **organic matter** mixed in. **Good drainage** is essential. Direct sow every two weeks in spring, or sow in fall for earlier spring blooms. Mix the tiny seeds with fine sand for even sowing. Do not cover because the seeds need light for germination. Deadhead to prolong blooming.

Tips
Poppies work well in mixed borders. They will fill empty spaces early in the season, then die back over summer, leaving room for slower plants to fill in. Poppies can also be used in rock gardens, and the cut flowers look good in fresh arrangements.

Recommended
P. nudicaule (Iceland poppy), a short-lived perennial, bears red, orange, yellow, pink or white flowers in spring and early summer.

P. rhoeas (Flanders poppy, field poppy, corn poppy) forms a basal rosette of foliage above which flowers in a wide range of colors are borne on long stems.

P. rhoeas Shirley Series (above); *P. nudicaule* (below)

California poppy (Eschscholzia californica) is a close poppy relative that you may also want to consider planting. The flowers usually come in gorgeous sorbet shades of orange and yellow, though reds, pinks and white are also available.

Features: brightly colored flowers **Flower color:** red, pink, white, purple, yellow, orange **Height:** 24–36" **Spread:** 12"

Salvia
Salvia

S. *splendens* (above); S. *viridis* (below)

There are over 900 species of Salvia.

Salvias should be part of every annual garden. The attractive and varied forms have something to offer every style of garden.

Growing
All salvia plants prefer **full sun** but tolerate light shade. The soil should be **moist** and **well drained** and of **average to rich fertility,** with a lot of **organic matter**.

Tips
Salvias look good grouped in beds and borders and in containers. The flowers are long lasting and make good cut flowers for arrangements.

To keep plants producing flowers, water often and fertilize monthly.

Recommended
S. coccinea (Texas sage) is a bushy, upright plant that bears whorled spikes of white, pink, blue or purple flowers. *S. farinacea* (mealy cup sage, blue sage) has bright blue flowers clustered along stems powdered with silver. Cultivars are available. *S. splendens* (salvia, scarlet sage) is grown for its spikes of bright red, tubular flowers. Recently, cultivars have become available in white, pink, purple and orange. *S. viridis* (*S. horminium*; annual clary sage) is grown for its colorful pink, purple, blue or white bracts, not its flowers.

Also called: sage **Features:** colorful summer flowers; attractive foliage **Flower color:** red, blue, purple, burgundy, pink, orange, salmon, yellow, cream, white, bicolored **Height:** 8"–4' **Spread:** 8"–4'

Snapdragon
Antirrhinum

Snapdragons are among the most appealing plants. The flower colors are always rich and vibrant, and even the most jaded gardeners are tempted to squeeze open the dragons' mouths.

Growing

Snapdragons prefer **full sun** but tolerate light or partial shade. The soil should be **fertile, rich in organic matter** and **well drained**. They prefer a **neutral or alkaline** soil and will not perform as well in acidic soil. Do not cover seeds when sowing; they require light for germination.

To encourage bushy growth, pinch the tips of the young plants. Cut off the flower spikes as they fade to promote further blooming and to prevent the plant from dying back before the end of the season.

Tips

The height of the variety dictates the best place for it in a border— the shortest varieties work well near the front, and the tallest look good in the center or back. The dwarf and medium-height varieties can also be used in planters. A trailing variety does well in hanging baskets.

Recommended

There are many cultivars of **A. majus** available, generally grouped into three size categories: dwarf, medium and giant.

A. *majus* cultivars (above & below)

Snapdragons may self-sow, but the hybrids will not come true to type.

Features: entertaining summer flowers
Flower color: white, cream, yellow, orange, red, maroon, pink, purple, bicolored **Height:** 6"–4' **Spread:** 6–24"

Sunflower

Helianthus

H. annuus (above & below)

Birds will flock to the ripening seedheads of your sunflowers and quickly pluck out the tightly packed seeds. Make sure to clear away the empty hulls as a chemical they release inhibits the growth of some plants.

There are many sunflower options, and each one adds cheerful charm to any location. We have never seen a sunflower we didn't like.

Growing

Sunflower grows best in **full sun**. The soil should be of **average fertility, humus rich, moist** and **well drained**. Successive plantings from spring to early summer will prolong the blooming period.

The annual sunflower is an excellent plant for a child's garden. The seeds are big and easy to handle, and they germinate quickly. The plants grow continually upward, and their progress can be measured until the flower finally appears on top.

Tips

Lower-growing varieties can be used in beds, borders and containers. Tall varieties work well at the back of borders and make good screens or temporary hedges. The tallest varieties may need staking.

Recommended

H. annuus (common sunflower) has attractive cultivars in a wide range of heights, with single stems or branching habits. Flowers come in a variety of colors, in single to fully double forms.

Features: late-summer flowers; edible seeds
Flower color: most commonly yellow but also orange, red, brown, cream, bicolored; typically with brown, purple or rusty red centers
Height: 16" for dwarf varieties; giants up to 15' **Spread:** 12–24"

Sweet Alyssum
Lobularia

L. maritima cultivar (above & below)

Sweet alyssum is excellent for creating soft edges. It self-seeds and pops up along pathways and between stones late in the season to give summer a sweet sendoff.

Growing

Sweet alyssum prefers **full sun** but tolerates light shade. **Well-drained** soil of **average fertility** is preferred, but poor soil is tolerated. Sweet alyssum may die back a bit during the heat and humidity of summer. Trim it back and water it periodically to encourage new growth and more flowers when the weather cools.

Tips

Sweet alyssum creeps around rock gardens, over rock walls and along the edges of beds. It is an excellent choice for seeding into the cracks and crevices of walkways and between patio stones, and once established it readily reseeds. It is also good for filling in spaces between taller plants in borders and mixed containers.

Recommended

L. maritima forms a low, spreading mound of foliage. The entire plant appears to be covered in tiny blossoms when in full flower. Cultivars with flowers in a wide range of colors are available.

Leave alyssum plants out all winter. In spring, remove the previous year's growth to expose self-sown seedlings below.

Features: fragrant flowers **Flower color:** pink, purple, yellow, salmon, white **Height:** 3–12" **Spread:** 6–24"

Verbena

Verbena

V. bonariensis (above); V. x hybrida (below)

The Romans, it is said, believed verbena could rekindle the flames of dying love. They named it Herba Veneris, *'plant of Venus.'*

Verbenas offer butterflies a banquet. Butterfly visitors include tiger swallowtails, silver-spotted skippers, great spangled fritillaries and painted ladies.

Growing

Verbenas grow best in **full sun**. The soil should be **fertile** and very **well drained**. Pinch back young plants for bushy growth.

Tips

Use verbenas on rock walls and in beds, borders, rock gardens, containers, hanging baskets and window boxes. They make good substitutes for ivy-leaved geraniums. Plant them in an area where the sun is hot or where a roof overhang can keep the mildew-prone verbenas dry.

Recommended

V. bonariensis is a tender perennial that is often grown as an annual. It forms a low clump of foliage from which tall, stiff stems bear clusters of small, purple flowers.

V. x *hybrida* is a bushy plant that may be upright or spreading. It bears clusters of small flowers in a wide range of colors. Cultivars are available.

Also called: garden verbena **Features:** summer flowers **Flower color:** red, pink, purple, blue, yellow, scarlet, silver, peach, white; some with white centers **Height:** 8"–5' **Spread:** 12–36"

Baby's Breath
Gypsophila

The airy, little flowers of this delicate perennial are the perfect accent to bold blossoms in fresh or dried arrangements, and in the garden.

Growing

Plant baby's breath in **full sun**. The soil must be **neutral** or **alkaline**, of **average fertility** and very **well drained**. Baby's breath easily rots in areas with moist, acidic soil.

Tips

Baby's breath ties together other plantings in the border with its cloud-like flower clusters.

Deadhead baby's breath to prolong the flowering period. This sounds easy enough to do but is a bit more difficult when the plant is covered in tiny blooms, all in different stages of development. Instead of trying to remove the faded flowers, wait until the entire plant is almost finished flowering; then, shear the entire plant back lightly to encourage new growth and a second flush of blooms later in the season.

Baby's breath will develop a large, thick taproot that should not be disturbed once it is established. There is no need to divide this plant.

Recommended

G. paniculata (common baby's breath) produces an upright, airy mound of tiny, white blossoms with dark green leaves. **'Pink Fairy'** bears pink flowers.

G. repens is a low-growing spreader with bluish green foliage and small, star-shaped flowers. Both the species and varied cultivars offer flower shades of pink, purple and white.

G. repens (above); *G. paniculata* with 'Stargazer Lily' (below)

Gypsophila comes from the words gypsos, or 'lime, gypsum,' and philos, 'loving,' referring to the plant's preference for chalky soils.

Features: tiny, airy flowers; habit; uses **Flower color:** pink, purple, white **Height:** 4–36" **Spread:** 12–36" **Hardiness:** zones 2–8

Bee Balm
Monarda

M. didyma 'Marshall's Delight' (above), M. didyma (below)

The fragrant flowers of bee balm are enticing to our senses of taste and smell and intoxicating to butterflies and bees.

Growing

Bee balm grows well in **full sun**, **partial shade** or **light shade**. The soil should be of **average fertility**, **humus rich**, **moist** and **well drained**.

Dry conditions encourage mildew and loss of leaves, so regular watering is a must. Divide every two or three years in spring as new growth emerges. In June, cut back some stems by half to extend the flowering period and encourage compact growth. Thinning the stems in spring also helps prevent powdery mildew. If mildew strikes after flowering, cut plants back to 6" to increase air circulation.

Tips

Use bee balm beside a stream or pond, or in a lightly shaded, well-watered border. It will spread in moist, fertile soils, but as with most mint species, bee balm roots are close to the surface and can be removed easily.

The fresh or dried leaves may be used to make a refreshing, minty, citrus-scented tea. Put a handful of fresh leaves in a teapot, pour boiling water over them and let steep for at least five minutes. Sweeten with honey to taste.

Bee balm attracts bees, butterflies and hummingbirds to the garden. Avoid using pesticides, which can seriously harm or kill these creatures and which will prevent you from using the plant for culinary or medicinal purposes.

Recommended

M. didyma is a bushy, mounding plant that forms a thick clump of stems with red or pink flowers. Many cultivars are available in varied colors, sizes and levels of mildew resistance.

Also called: bergamot, Oswego tea
Features: fragrant, colorful blossoms
Flower color: red, pink **Height:** 2–4'
Spread: 12–24" **Hardiness:** zones 3–8

Bellflower

Campanula

C. medium (above); C. carpatica 'White Clips' (below)

hanks to their wide range of heights and habits, it is possible to put bellflowers almost anywhere in the garden.

Growing

Bellflowers grow well in **full sun, partial shade** or **light shade**. The soil should be of **average to high fertility** and **well drained**. Mulch to keep roots cool and moist in summer and protected in winter, particularly if snow cover is inconsistent. Deadhead to prolong blooming.

Tips

Plant upright and mounding bellflowers in borders and cottage gardens. Use low, spreading and trailing bellflowers in rock gardens and on rock walls. You can also edge beds with the low-growing varieties.

Recommended

C. carpatica (Carpathian bellflower, Carpathian harebell) is a spreading, mounding perennial that bears blue, white or purple flowers in summer. Several cultivars are available.

C. glomerata (clustered bellflower) forms a clump of upright stems and bears clusters of purple, blue or white flowers most of summer.

C. medium (Canterbury bells) is an upright biennial plant with narrow leaves and bell-shaped flowers with recurved edges. Dwarf cultivars and double forms are available.

C. persicifolia (peach-leaved bellflower) is an upright perennial that bears white, blue or purple flowers from early to mid-summer.

Divide bellflowers every few years, in early spring or late summer, to keep plants vigorous and to prevent them from becoming invasive.

Features: spring, summer or autumn flowers; varied growing habits **Flower color:** blue, white, purple, pink **Height:** 4–36" **Spread:** 12–24" **Hardiness:** zones 3–7

Bitterroot
Lewisia

Bitterroot blossoms are a sight worth waiting for, featuring tiny flowers you can bring indoors for all to see.

Growing

Grow bitterroot in **full sun**. The soil should be **moderately fertile**, **humus rich**, **neutral** or **acidic** and very **well drained**. Allow bitterroot to dry out after blooming—it may require protection from heavy rain.

Tips

Bitterroot is the perfect plant for dry, exposed areas such as in the crevices of a rock wall, rock garden, trough and hypertufa gardens or dry banks. It does not need dividing.

The small offsets that develop at the base of the plant may be separated in early summer and rooted in pots. Grow the young plants in pots for a year before planting them in the garden. Mulch with gravel to keep excess moisture away from the fleshy leaves.

Recommended

L. rediviva forms low-growing tufts of club-shaped foliage that dies back either during or soon after flowering. Funnel-shaped flowers, made up of 12–19 narrow petals just above the leaves, emerge from early spring to summer.

Features: succulent foliage; colorful flowers
Flower color: pink, white **Height:** 2–4"
Spread: 2–4" **Hardiness:** zones 4–8

Black-Eyed Susan

Rudbeckia

Black-eyed Susan is a tough, low maintenance, long-lived perennial. Plant it wherever you want a casual look. Black-eyed Susan looks great planted in drifts.

Growing

Black-eyed Susan grows well in **full sun** or **partial shade**. The soil should be of **average fertility** and **well drained**. Several *Rudbeckia* species are touted as 'claybusters' because they tolerate fairly heavy clay soils. Established plants are drought tolerant but regular watering is best. Divide in spring or fall, every three to five years.

Tips

Include these native plants in wildflower and natural gardens, beds and borders. Pinching the plants in June will result in shorter, bushier stands.

R. fulgida (above)

Recommended

*R. **fulgida*** is an upright, spreading plant bearing orange-yellow flowers with brown centers. **Var. *sullivantii* 'Gold-sturm'** bears large, bright, golden yellow flowers.

*R. **laciniata*** (cutleaf coneflower) forms a large, open clump. The yellow flowers have green centers. **'Goldquelle'** has bright yellow, double flowers.

The cut flowers are long-lasting in arrangements.

Features: bright flowers; attractive foliage; easy to grow **Flower color:** yellow, orange or red, with centers typically brown or green **Height:** 2–6' **Spread:** 18–36" **Hardiness:** zones 3–8

Bleeding Heart
Dicentra

D. spectabilis (above & below)

Every garden should have a bleeding heart. Tucked away in a shady spot, this lovely plant reappears each spring and fills the garden with fresh promise.

These delicate plants are the perfect addition to a moist woodland garden. Plant them next to a shaded pond or stream.

Growing
Bleeding hearts prefer **light shade** but tolerate partial or full shade. The soil should be **humus rich, moist** and **well drained**. These plants die back in very dry summers but revive in autumn or the following spring. Bleeding hearts must remain moist while blooming to prolong the flowering period. Regular watering keeps flowers coming until mid-summer. *D. exima* and *D. spectabilis* rarely need dividing. *D. formosa* can be divided every three years or so.

Tips
Bleeding hearts can be naturalized in a woodland garden or grown in a border or rock garden. They make excellent early-season specimen plants and do well near ponds or streams.

All bleeding hearts contain toxic alkaloids, and some people develop allergic skin reactions from contact with these plants.

Recommended
D. eximia (fringed bleeding heart) forms a loose, mounded clump of lacy, fern-like foliage and bears pink or white flowers in spring and sporadically over summer.

D. spectabilis (common bleeding heart, Japanese bleeding heart) forms a large, elegant mound that bears flowers with white inner petals and pink outer petals. Several cultivars are available.

Features: spring and summer flowers; attractive foliage **Flower color:** pink, white, red, purple **Height:** 8–36" **Spread:** 12–24" **Hardiness:** zones 3–8

Columbine
Aquilegia

Delicate and beautiful columbines add a touch of simple elegance to any garden. Blooming from spring to mid-summer, these long-lasting flowers herald the passing of cool spring weather and the arrival of summer.

Growing

Columbines grow well in **light shade** or **partial shade**. They prefer soil that is **fertile, moist** and **well drained**, but they adapt to most soil conditions. Division is not required but can be done to propagate desirable plants. Divided plants may take time to recover because columbines dislike having their roots disturbed.

Tips

Use columbines in rock gardens, formal or casual borders and naturalized or woodland gardens. Place them where other plants can fill in to hide the foliage as the columbines die back over summer.

If leaf miners are a problem, cut the foliage back once flowering is complete, and new foliage will fill in.

Recommended

A. canadensis (wild columbine, Canada columbine) is a native plant that is common in woodlands and fields. It bears yellow flowers with red spurs.

A. x *hybrida* (*A.* x *cultorum*; hybrid columbine) forms mounds of delicate foliage and has exceptional flowers. Many hybrids have been developed with showy flowers in a wide range of colors.

A. canadensis (above); A. x hybrida 'McKana Giant' (below)

A. vulgaris (European columbine, common columbine) has been used to develop many hybrids and cultivars with flowers in a variety of colors and forms, including double-flowered cultivars that look like frilly dahlias.

Columbines self-seed but are not invasive. Each year a few new seedlings may turn up near the parent plant and can be transplanted.

Features: spring and summer flowers; attractive foliage **Flower color:** red, yellow, pink, purple, blue, white; color of spurs often differs from that of the petals **Height:** 18–36" **Spread:** 12–24" **Hardiness:** zones 3–8

Coral Bells

Heuchera

H. sanguinea (above & below)

From soft yellow-greens and oranges to midnight purples and silvery, dappled maroons, coral bells offer a great variety of foliage options for a perennial garden with partial shade.

Growing

Coral bells grow best in **light or partial shade**. The foliage colors can bleach out in full sun, and plants grow leggy in full shade. The soil should be of **average to rich fertility, humus rich, neutral to alkaline, moist** and **well drained**. Good air circulation is essential. Deadhead to prolong the bloom.

Every two or three years, coral bells should be dug up and the oldest, woodiest roots and stems removed. Plants may be divided at this time, if desired, then replanted with the crown at or just above soil level.

Tips

Use coral bells as edging plants or in clusters in woodland gardens; in low traffic areas, use them as groundcovers. Combine different foliage types for an interesting display.

Recommended

H. sanguinea (red coral bells) produces a mound of small, rounded leaves that are often deep green, occasionally mottled with silver or variegated. Tiny, red flowers emerge through the foliage on tall, wiry stems. Many cultivars are available in varied forms, leaf colors and patterns.

Also called: heuchera, alum root **Features:** very decorative foliage; spring or summer flowers **Flower color:** red, pink, white, yellow, purple; also grown for foliage **Height:** 12–30" **Spread:** 6–18" **Hardiness:** zones 4–9

Daylily
Hemerocallis

The daylily's adaptability and durability combined with its variety of colors, blooming periods, sizes and textures explain this perennial's popularity.

Growing

Daylilies grow in any light from **full sun to full shade**. The deeper the shade, the fewer flowers will be produced. The soil should be **fertile, moist** and **well drained**, but these plants adapt to most conditions and are hard to kill once established. Divide every two to three years to keep plants vigorous and to propagate them. They can, however, be left indefinitely without dividing.

Tips

Plant daylilies alone, or group them in borders, on banks and in ditches to control erosion. They can be naturalized in woodland or meadow gardens. Small varieties are nice in planters.

Deadhead to prolong the blooming period. Be careful when deadheading purple-flowered daylilies because the sap can stain fingers and clothes.

Recommended

Daylilies come in an almost infinite number of forms, sizes and colors in a range of species, cultivars and hybrids. See your local garden center or daylily grower to find out what's available and most suitable for your garden.

'Dewey Roquemore' (above); 'Bonanza' (below)

The petals of daylily are edible. Add them to salads for a splash of color and a pleasantly peppery taste.

Features: spring and summer flowers; grass-like foliage **Flower color:** every color, except blue and pure white **Height:** 12"–4' **Spread:** 12"–4' **Hardiness:** zones 3–9

Dead Nettle
Lamium

L. maculatum 'Limelight' (above); *L.m.* 'Beacon Silver' (below)

These attractive plants, with their striped, dotted or banded silver and green foliage, hug the ground and thrive on only the barest necessities of life.

Growing

Dead nettles prefer **partial to light shade**. They tolerate full sun but may become leggy. The soil should be of **average fertility, humus rich, moist** and **well drained**. The more fertile the soil, the more vigorously the plants will grow. They are drought tolerant in shade but develop bare patches if the soil dries out for extended periods. Divide and replant in autumn if bare spots become unsightly.

Dead nettles remain more compact if sheared back after flowering. If they remain green over the winter, shear back in early spring.

Tips

These plants make useful groundcovers for woodland or shade gardens. They also help keep weeds down under shrubs in a border.

Recommended

L. album (white deadnettle, archangel) is an upright perennial with solid green foliage and bears white flowers in early spring.

L. maculatum (spotted dead nettle) is the most commonly grown dead nettle. This low-growing, spreading species has green leaves with white or silvery markings and bears white, pink or mauve flowers. Many cultivars are available.

Also called: spotted dead nettle, lamium
Features: spring or summer flowers; decorative, often variegated foliage **Flower color:** white, pink, yellow, mauve; also grown for foliage **Height:** 6–24" **Spread:** 12–24" **Hardiness:** zones 2–8

Delphinium
Delphinium

Delphinium is the royalty of the perennial border. Tall, bold and astounding in bloom, the delphinium reminds us what growing flowers is all about.

Growing
Grow delphiniums in a **full sun** location that is well protected from strong winds. The soil should be **fertile**, **moist** and **humus rich** with **excellent drainage**.

Tips
Delphiniums are classic cottage garden plants. Their height and need for staking relegate them to the back of the border, where they make a magnificent backdrop for warmer foreground flowers such as peonies, poppies and black-eyed Susans.

Recommended
D. x *belladonna* (belladonna hybrids) bear flowers of blue, white or mauve in loose, branched spikes. They grow over 36" tall and almost 24" wide.

D. x *elatum* (elatum hybrids) bear densely held flowers of blue, purple, white, pink or yellow on tall spikes. They are divided into three height categories—dwarfs, mediums and talls—ranging in height from 5–6$^1/_2$' tall.

D. grandiflorum bears flowers of blue, purple or white in loose, branched clusters. It grows up to 24" tall and 12" wide.

D. x belladonna hybrid (above); *D. x elatum* hybrid (below)

These plants are so gorgeous in bloom that you can build a garden or plan a party around their flowering.

Features: tall, spiky clusters of colorful flowers; ornate foliage **Flower color:** blue, purple, pink, white, bicolored **Height:** 2–6½' **Spread:** 3½–40" **Hardiness:** zones 3–7

Elephant Ears
Bergenia

B. cordifolia (above)

B. cordifolia is also known as pigsqueak, giant rockfoil, heart-leaf bergenia and leather-leaf rockfoil.

The reawakening of elephant ears is a sure sign of spring. The leaves only fade and collapse a little throughout the winter months, but once the snow melts in spring, they rise back up, take shape and the plants bloom.

Growing

Elephant ears grows best in **partial shade**. The soil should be of **average to rich fertility** and **well drained**. A moist soil is preferable, especially when plants are grown in sunnier areas. However, elephant ears is fairly drought tolerant once established.

Tips

Versatile and low-growing, these plants can be used as groundcovers, as edging along borders and pathways, as part of woodland rock gardens and in mass plantings under trees and shrubs.

Recommended

B. cordifolia produces rounded, leathery leaves that form dense clusters. The leaves turn a reddish shade of bronze in fall. Purplish flower stems rise through the foliage tipped with clusters of pink flowers in early spring. Cultivars are available with varied flower and foliage color.

Features: evergreen foliage; complementary flowers **Flower color:** white, red, purple, light to dark pink **Height:** 24" **Spread:** 24" or more **Hardiness:** zones 3–8

Gayfeather

Liatris

Gayfeather is an outstanding cut flower with fuzzy, spiked blossoms above grass-like foliage. This native wildflower is an excellent plant for attracting butterflies to the garden.

Growing
Gayfeather prefers **full sun**. The soil should be of **average fertility, sandy** and **humus rich**. Water well during the growing season but don't allow the plants to stand in water during cool weather. Mulch during summer to prevent moisture loss. Established plants are quite drought tolerant.

Trim off the spent flower spikes to promote a longer blooming period and to keep gayfeather looking tidy. Spikes can be left on the plant to the end of the flowering season for winter interest. This plant self seeds, but seedlings may not be identical to the parent plants.

Tips
Use this plant in borders and meadow plantings where the tall, flowering spikes will create a striking contrast with other perennials and shrubs. Plant in a location that has good drainage to avoid root-rot in winter. Gayfeather grows well in planters.

Recommended
L. spicata is a clump-forming, erect plant with pinkish purple or white flowers. Several cultivars are available.

***

Features: summer flowers; grass-like foliage **Flower color:** purple, white **Height:** 18–36" **Spread:** 18–24" **Hardiness:** zones 3–9

L. spicata 'Kobold' (above); *L. spicata* (below)

The spikes make excellent, long-lasting cut flowers. Plants can be divided every three to five years when the clump starts to look crowded.

Globe Flower
Trollius

T. x cultorum 'Golden Queen' (above); *T. x cultorum* (below)

Globe flowers are also known as buttercups, and a few of the species bear flowers that resemble yellow cabbage roses.

Yellow flowers bring such joy and color to the garden, and globe flowers are no exception.

Growing

Globe flowers prefer **partial shade** but tolerate full sun if enough moisture is provided. Plants prefer cool, moist conditions and do not tolerate drought. The soil should be **fertile** and **heavy** and not be allowed to dry out. Globe flowers can be planted in **well-drained** soil as long as the soil remains moist. Prune out any yellowing leaves in summer. Division is rarely required but can be done in early spring or late fall.

Tips

Globe flower is the perfect plant for the side of a pond or stream. It will naturalize very well in a damp meadow garden or bog garden and can be used in a border as long as the soil remains moist. Globe flowers are long lasting as cut flowers.

Recommended

T. asiaticus produces divided leaves and rich golden-yellow flowers. **'Giganteus'** shares similarities to the species but is a more substantial form.

T. x *cultorum* **hybrids** (hybrid globe flower) forms perfectly globe-shaped flowers on low mounds of lush, ornate foliage. Many cultivars are available in fiery shades and varied sizes.

T. pumilus (dwarf globeflower) is a low-growing rock garden or edging variety with single, bright yellow flowers that are small compared to other species and are borne atop a low mound of shiny foliage.

Features: blossoms; ornate foliage **Flower color:** bright yellow, orange **Height:** 12–36" **Spread:** 18–24" **Hardiness:** zones: 3–7

Hollyhock

Alcea

Nothing says 'storybook charm' like hollyhocks against a picket fence or stone wall, gently waving in warm summer breezes, tall and proud.

Growing

Hollyhocks prefer to grow in **full sun** but tolerate partial shade. The soil should be **average to rich** and **well drained**. New daughter plants that develop around the base of the mature plant may be divided off in order to propagate fancy or desirable specimens. They don't always come true to type from seed, so this may be the only way to get more of a plant that is particularly attractive.

Tips

Because they are so tall, hollyhocks look best at the back of a border or in the center of an island bed. They will get some support from a fence if placed up against it. If hollyhocks are planted in any windy location they will need to be staked.

Hollyhocks can be grown shorter and bushier with smaller flowers if the main stem is pinched out early in the season. These shorter flower stems are less likely to be broken by the wind and therefore can be left unstaked.

Old-fashioned hollyhocks typically have single flowers and grow much taller than newer hybrids but are more disease resistant. Growing them as biennials and removing them after they flower is a good way to keep rust at bay.

A. rosea

Features: tall architectural form; colorful flowers
Flower color: yellow, white, apricot, pink, red, purple, reddish black **Height:** 5–8'
Spread: 24" **Hardiness:** zones 3–8

Recommended

A. rosea forms a rosette of leaves with tall, flowering stalks bearing ruffled single or double blooms.

A. rugosa (Russian hollyhock) is similar to *A. rosea* but is more resistant to hollyhock rust. It bears pale yellow to orangy yellow, single flowers.

Iris
Iris

I. sibirica (above); *I.* x *germanica* hybrid (below)

Irises are steeped in history and lore. Many say the range in flower colors of bearded irises approximates that of a rainbow.

Growing

Irises prefer **full sun** but tolerate very light or dappled shade. The soil should be of **average fertility** and **well drained**. Japanese iris and Siberian iris prefer a moist but still well-drained soil.

Divide in late summer or after flowering. When dividing bearded iris rhizomes, replant with the flat side of the foliage fan facing the garden.

Deadhead irises to keep them tidy. Cut the foliage back in spring or fall along with your other perennials.

Tips

Irises are popular border plants; Japanese iris and Siberian iris are also useful alongside streams or ponds. Dwarf cultivars are attractive in rock gardens.

Wash your hands after handling irises because iris tissue can cause severe internal irritation if ingested. Do not plant irises close to children's play areas.

Recommended

Among the most popular of the many species and hybrids is the bearded iris, often a hybrid of **I.** x ***germanica***. It has the widest range of flower colors but is susceptible to the iris borer, which can kill the plant. Several irises are not susceptible, including Japanese iris (**I. ensata**), dwarf bearded iris (**I. pumila**) and Siberian iris (**I. sibirica**).

Features: spring, summer and sometimes autumn flowers; attractive foliage **Flower color:** many shades of pink, red, purple, blue, white, brown, yellow **Height:** 8"–4' **Spread:** 6"–4' **Hardiness:** zones 2–8

Lamb's Ears

Stachys

S. byzantina 'Big Ears' (above); *S. byzantina* (below)

The soft, fuzzy leaves of lamb's ears give this perennial its common name. The silvery foliage is a beautiful contrast to bold-colored plants that tower above; it softens hard lines and surfaces.

Growing
Lamb's ears grows best in **full sun**. The soil should be of **poor or average fertility** and **well drained**. The leaves can rot in humid weather if the soil is poorly drained. Remove spent flower spikes to keep plants looking neat.

Tips
Lamb's ears makes a great groundcover in a new garden where the soil has not yet been amended. It can be used to edge borders and pathways because it provides a soft, silvery backdrop for more vibrant colors in the border. For a silvery accent, plant a small group of lamb's ears in a border.

Recommended
S. byzantina forms a mat of thick, woolly rosettes of leaves. Pinkish purple flowers bloom all summer. There are many cultivars that offer a variety of foliage colors, sizes and flowers.

Also called: lamb's tails, lamb's tongues
Features: soft, fuzzy, silver foliage **Flower color:** pink, purple **Height:** 6–18" **Spread:** 18–24" **Hardiness:** zones 3–8

Lily-of-the-Valley
Convallaria

C. majalis (above & below)

rich and moist, but almost any soil condition is tolerated. This plant is drought resistant.

Division is rarely required but can be done whenever you need plants for another area or want to donate to someone else's garden. Pairs of leaves grow from small pips, or eyes, that form along the spreading rhizome. Divide a length of root into pieces, leaving at least one pip on each piece.

Tips
This versatile groundcover can be grown in a variety of locations. Lily-of-the-valley is a good plant to naturalize in woodland gardens, perhaps bordering a pathway or beneath shade trees where little else will grow. It also makes a good groundcover in a shrub border, where its dense growth and fairly shallow roots will keep the weeds down but won't interfere with the shrubs' roots.

Lily-of-the-valley can be quite invasive. It is a good idea not to grow it with plants that are less vigorous and likely to be overwhelmed, such as alpine plants in a shady rock garden. Give lily-of-the-valley plenty of space to grow and let it go. Avoid planting it in a place where you may later spend all your time trying to get rid of it.

Recommended
C. majalis forms a mat of foliage. In spring it produces small, arching stems lined with fragrant, white, bell-shaped flowers. Many cultivars are available bearing either white or pink, nodding blossoms.

The dainty bells of lily-of-the-valley possess a heady scent. The flowers are sometimes hidden within the folded leaves, and it isn't until you walk by and detect the sweet perfume wafting past that you think to look for them.

Growing
Lily-of-the-valley grows well in any light from **full sun to full shade**. The soil should ideally be of **average fertility, humus**

Features: habit; flowers; foliage **Flower color:** white, pink **Height:** 6–12" **Spread:** indefinite **Hardiness:** zones 2–7

Lupine
Lupinus

Russell hybrids

$\mathcal{S}$eeing large plantings of lupines is an experience not soon forgotten; the flower colors blend from one shade to another like melting ice cream.

Growing

Grow these plants in **full sun** or **partial shade**. The soil should be **average to fairly fertile**, **sandy, well drained** and **slightly acidic**. Protect lupines from drying winds. Lupines don't like to have their roots disturbed.

The small offsets that develop at the base of lupines may be carefully separated and replanted to propagate the plant.

Features: attractive, colorful flower spikes; ornate foliage **Flower color:** white, cream, yellow, pink, red, orange, purple, blue; often bicolored **Height:** 12–36" **Spread:** 12–18" **Hardiness:** zones 4–6

Tips

Lupines are wonderful when massed together in borders or in cottage or natural gardens. Deadheading is recommended to encourage more flower spikes later in the season. However, lupines may self-seed if the spent spikes are left in place. Leave a few spikes in place after the flowers are gone if you want to have some new plants to replace the older ones that die out.

Recommended

Russell hybrids (Russell lupines) are a group of hybrids developed from crossing several species of lupines. The result is this popular dwarf group, which bears flowers in a wide range of solid colors and bicolors.

Penstemon

Penstemon

P. digitalis 'Husker Red'

Penstemons require well-drained soil, but at the same time they prefer even moisture and a bit of compost in spring and fall.

Penstemon's colorful stalks will welcome hummingbirds and butterflies on a summer day.

Growing

Penstemons prefer **full sun** but tolerate some shade. The soil should be of **average to rich fertility, sandy** and **well drained**. Penstemons are drought tolerant but will rot in wet soil. Plant in spring or fall; divide every two or three years in spring.

To support the tall stems, insert twiggy branches around the plants in spring before they grow too tall. Pinch plants when they reach a height of 12" to encourage bushy growth.

Tips

The attractive flowers make a lovely addition to a mixed border, cottage garden or rock garden.

Recommended

Penstemon has many species, cultivars and hybrids, which provide a range of flower colors, shapes and sizes. Check your local garden center or nursery to see what is available.

P. digitalis '**Husker Red**' is a recent Perennial Plant Association Perennial Plant of the Year. The bronzed-red foliage contrasts well with its white flowers.

Also called: beard tongue **Features:** interesting flowers **Flower color:** white, yellow, light pink, rose pink, purple **Height:** 8–24" **Spread:** 10–12" **Hardiness:** zones 4–8

Peony
Paeonia

Once the fleeting, but magnificent, peony flower display is done, the foliage remains stellar throughout the growing season.

Growing

Peonies prefer **full sun** but tolerate some shade. The planting site should be well prepared with **fertile, humus-rich, moist, well-drained** soil with a lot of compost. Mulch peonies lightly with compost in spring. Too much fertilizer, particularly nitrogen, causes floppy growth and retards blooming. Division is not required but can be done in autumn to propagate plants. Deadhead to keep plants looking tidy.

Tips

Combine peonies in a border with other early bloomers. Underplant them with bulbs—when the bulbs die down by mid-summer, the emerging peony foliage will hide their dying foliage. Avoid planting peonies under trees, where they will compete for moisture and nutrients.

Tubers planted too shallowly or, more commonly, too deeply, will not flower. The buds or eyes on the tuber should be 1–2" below the soil surface.

P. lactiflora 'Shimmering Velvet' (above); *P. lactiflora* cultivars (below)

Place wire tomato or peony cages around the plants in early spring to support the heavy flowers. The foliage will grow into the wires and hide the cage.

Recommended

There are hundreds of peonies available. Cultivars come in a wide range of colors, may have single or double flowers, and may or may not be fragrant. Visit your local garden center to check for availability.

Features: spring and early-summer flowers; attractive foliage **Flower color:** white, cream white, yellow, pink, red, purple **Height:** 24–32" **Spread:** 24–32" **Hardiness:** zones 2–8

Phlox

Phlox

P. paniculata (above & below)

The many species of phlox can be found in varied climates, from dry, exposed mountainsides, to moist, sheltered woodlands.

Phlox comes in many shapes and sizes, from low creepers to bushy border plants, with flowering periods falling anywhere between early spring and mid-autumn.

Growing

P. paniculata and *P. maculata* prefer **full sun**; *P. subulata* prefers **full sun to partial shade**; and *P. stolonifera* prefers **light to partial shade** but tolerates heavy shade. All prefer **fertile, humus-rich, moist, well-drained** soil. Divide in autumn or spring.

Tips

Low-growing species are useful in rock gardens or at the front of borders. Taller phloxes may be used in the middle of borders and are particularly effective if planted in groups.

Recommended

P. maculata (early phlox, garden phlox, wild sweet William) forms an upright clump of hairy stems and narrow leaves that are sometimes spotted with red. Pink, purple or white flowers are borne in conical clusters.

P. paniculata (garden phlox, summer phlox) is an upright plant. The many cultivars vary in size and flower color.

P. stolonifera (creeping phlox) is a low, spreading plant that bears flowers in several shades of purple.

P. subulata (moss phlox, moss pink) is very low growing and bears flowers in various colors. The foliage is evergreen.

Features: spring, summer or autumn flowers **Flower color:** white, blue, purple, orange, pink, red **Height:** 2"–4' **Spread:** 12–36" **Hardiness:** zones 3–8

Pinks
Dianthus

D. deltoides (above); *D. plumarius* (below)

From tiny and delicate to large and robust, this genus contains a wide variety of plants, many with spice-scented flowers.

Growing

Pinks prefer **full sun** but tolerate some light shade. A **well-drained, neutral or alkaline** soil is required. The most important factor is drainage—pinks hate to stand in water. Rocky outcroppings make up the native habitat of many species.

Tips

Pinks are excellent for rock gardens and rock walls, and for edging flower borders and walkways. They can also be used in cutting gardens and even as groundcovers. To prolong blooming, deadhead as the flowers fade, but leave a few flowers to go to seed.

Features: sometimes-fragrant spring or summer flowers; attractive foliage **Flower color:** pink, red, white, purple **Height:** 6–12" **Spread:** 8–18" **Hardiness:** zones 2–8

Recommended

D. x ***allwoodii*** (allwood pinks) is a hybrid that forms a compact mound and bears flowers in a wide range of colors. Many cultivars are available.

*D. **deltoides*** (maiden pink) forms a mat of foliage with flowers in shades of red.

*D. **gratianopolitanus*** (cheddar pink) is long-lived and forms a very dense mat of evergreen, silver gray foliage with sweet-scented flowers mostly in shades of pink.

*D. **plumarius*** (cottage pink) is noteworthy for its role in the development of many popular cultivars known collectively as garden pinks. The flowers can be single, semi-double or fully double and are available in many colors.

Prairie Coneflower
Echinacea

'Magnus' & 'White Swan' (above); *E. purpurea* (below)

Prairie coneflower is a native wild-flower renowned for its medicinal value and the visual delight it creates in the landscape, with its pinkish purple petals encircling spiky, orange centers.

Growing

Prairie coneflower grows well in **full sun** or very **light shade**. It tolerates any **well-drained** soil but prefers an **average to rich** soil. Its thick taproot makes this plant drought resistant, but it prefers to have regular water. Divide every four years or so in spring or autumn.

Deadhead early in the season to prolong flowering. Later you may wish to leave the flowerheads in place to self-seed and provide winter interest. Pinch plants back or thin out the stems in early June to encourage bushy growth that is less prone to mildew. This will also encourage a later but longer blooming period.

Tips

Plant prairie coneflowers in meadow gardens and informal borders, either in groups or as single specimens. Prairie coneflower combines well with ornamental grasses and blue- or yellow-flowered perennials and shrubs.

Recommended

E. purpurea is an upright plant covered in prickly hairs. It bears pinkish purple flowers with conical, orangy centers, and it has several cultivars: **'Magnus,'** the 1998 Perennial Plant of the Year, has purple petals that stand out from the central cone; **'Razzmatazz'** has bright pink petals and a pompom-like flower form; and **'White Swan'** has white petals.

Also called: coneflower, purple coneflower
Features: mid-summer to autumn flowers; persistent seedheads **Flower color:** purple, pink, white; rusty orange centers **Height:** 2–5'
Spread: 12–24" **Hardiness:** zones 3–8

Prairie Smoke

Geum

G. *quellyon* (above), G. *coccineum* (below)

Prairie smoke will find a place in more gardens as its easy ways and plentiful warm flowers earn it the popularity it deserves.

Growing

Plant prairie smoke in a location that receives **full sun** but doesn't get too hot. The soil should be **fertile, evenly moist** and **well drained**. Prairie smoke does not like water-logged soil.

You will need to divide every year in spring or late summer because this plant can be short-lived.

Tips

Prairie smoke makes a brightly flowered addition to a border. It looks particularly attractive when combined with plants that have dark blue or purple flowers. Cut off spent flowers to keep more coming.

Also called: avens **Features:** flowers; foliage **Flower color:** orange, red, yellow, cream, pink **Height:** 6–24" **Spread:** 12–24" **Hardiness:** zones 4–8

Recommended

G. coccineum (*G.* x *borisii;* scarlet avens) forms a mounded clump of coarsely textured, rounded foliage. It bears bright, scarlet red flowers from late spring to late summer.

G. quellyon (*G. chiloense;* Chilean avens) forms a clump of foliage equally tall and wide, and it bears scarlet flowers all summer. '**Mrs. Bradshaw**' has orange-red flowers.

G. reptans is a spreading perennial bearing rosettes of coarsely textured, rounded leaves. It bears shallowly cupped, bright yellow flowers.

There are species of prairie smoke found in mountainous regions all over the world.

Primrose
Primula

P. x *polyantha* hybrids (above & below)

Plant primroses among dwarf daffodils, lungworts and pulmonarias; they complement this attractive tapestry of woodland flowers. Primroses are the jewels of the spring display.

Growing

Grow primrose in **partial shade,** in **moderately fertile, humus-rich, moist, well-drained, neutral to slightly acidic** soil. Overgrown clumps should be divided after flowering or in early fall. Plant in spring.

Pull off yellowing or dried leaves in fall to encourage fresh, new growth in spring.

Tips

Primroses work well in many areas of the garden; some prefer woodland areas while others thrive in moisture. Species with flowers on tall stems look excellent in masses, while species with solitary flowers peeking out among the foliage add an interesting dimension to the garden.

Recommended

The most popular primroses are **x polyantha hybrids**, which are available in a wide range of solid colors or bicolors. Many species and cultivars are available, with colorful flowers and a variety of plant forms.

Features: colorful flowers; variety of forms
Flower color: red, orange, pink, purple, blue, white, yellow **Height:** 6–24" **Spread:** 6–18"
Hardiness: zones 3–8

Sedum
Sedum

S. acre (above); *S. spectabile* hybrid (below)

Some 300–500 species of sedum are distributed throughout the Northern Hemisphere. Many sedums are grown for their foliage, which can range in color from steel gray-blue and green to red and burgundy.

Growing

Sedums prefer **full sun** but tolerate partial shade. The soil should be of **average fertility,** very **well drained** and **neutral to alkaline**. Divide in spring when needed.

Tips

Low-growing sedums make wonderful groundcovers and additions to rock gardens or rock walls. They also edge beds and borders beautifully. Taller sedums give a lovely late-season display in a bed or border.

Also called: stonecrop Features: summer to autumn flowers; decorative fleshy foliage Flower color: yellow, white, red, pink; also grown for foliage Height: 2–24" Spread: 12–24" or more Hardiness: zones 2–8

Recommended

S. acre (gold moss stonecrop) is a low-growing, wide-spreading plant that bears small, yellow-green flowers.

S. spectabile (showy stonecrop) is an upright species with pink flowers. Cultivars are available.

S. spurium (two-row stonecrop) forms a low, wide mat of foliage with deep pink or white flowers. Many cultivars are available and are often grown for their colorful foliage.

Snow-in-Summer
Cerastium

Snow-in-summer is a prolifically blooming perennial groundcover that is certain to perform regardless of soil conditions, parched places, slopes or neglect.

Growing
Grow snow-in-summer in **full sun** or **partial shade**. This plant will grow in any type of **well-drained** soil but may develop root-rot in wet soil. The richer the soil, the more invasive snow-in-summer becomes, but it tolerates poor soil.

Tips
Snow-in-summer is well suited to sunny, hot, well-drained locations and may be used under taller plants, as a ground cover, along border edges, or to prevent erosion on sloping banks. It is attractive in a rock wall, but its inva-siveness may overwhelm the often smaller and less vigorous plants that are popular in rock walls.

Cutting the plant back after it has fin-ished flowering and again later in sum-mer will help keep growth in check and prevent the plant from thinning out excessively in the center. Snow-in-summer tends to die out in the middle as it grows, so dividing it every two years will ensure that it maintains even coverage where you want it to.

Recommended
C. tomentosum is a low-growing groundcover bearing copious amounts of small, white, five-petaled flowers. The foliage is silvery white and covered in little hairs.

C. tomentosum (above & below)

Snow-in-summer contrasts dramatically with plants bearing green foliage and brightly colored flowers. It can spread 36" in a single year.

Features: carpet of flowers; silvery foliage; habit **Flower color:** white **Height:** 4–8"
Spread: indefinite **Hardiness:** zones 3–8

Alder

Alnus

Alders are related to birch trees and are equally as fond of permanently wet sites. These simple trees lack the bells and whistles of more ornate varieties, but they do provide shade to otherwise hot areas and adapt easily to infertile, poor or polluted soils.

Growing

Alders prefer **full sun**. The soil should be **consistently moist**, if not wet, and of **average to low fertility**.

Tips

Alders love sunlight and will not survive for long next to larger stands of trees or large structures that block the sunlight. Alders work well as shade trees.

Recommended

A great number of *Alnus* species are available, including a few cultivars. These upright, medium-sized trees often have arching branches, sharply toothed, textured leaves and decorative bark.

A. incana 'Pendula' (above); A. glutinosa (below)

Alders produce egg-shaped, female catkins that hang in groups at the branch tips.

A. incana (speckled alder, gray alder, white alder) is a tall, dense tree suitable for planting in wet areas, and **A. glutinosa** (black alder) produces dark, glossy leaves and dark brown, deeply furrowed bark. **A. tenuifolia** (thinleaf alder, mountain alder) is a smaller form with dark foliage and catkins that persist into winter, and **A. viridis** (mountain alder) is a smaller, low-headed specimen.

Features: habit; tolerance to moisture; hardiness **Habit:** open, upright, spreading tree **Height:** 10–40' **Spread:** 12–20' **Hardiness:** zones 3–7

Arborvitae
Thuja

T. occidentalis 'Yellow Ribbon' (above); T. occidentalis (below)

Deer enjoy eating the foliage of eastern arborvitae. Consider using western arborvitae, which is relatively resistant to deer browsing, instead.

Arborvitae are rot resistant, durable and long-lived, earning quiet admiration from gardeners everywhere.

Growing
Arborvitae prefer **full sun** but tolerate light to partial shade. The soil should be of **average fertility, moist** and **well drained**. These plants enjoy humidity and will perform best in a location with some shelter from wind, especially in winter, when the foliage can easily dry out and give the entire plant a rather brown, drab appearance.

Tips
Large varieties of arborvitae make excellent specimen trees, and smaller cultivars can be used in foundation plantings and shrub borders and as formal or informal hedges.

Recommended
T. occidentalis (eastern arborvitae, eastern white cedar) is a narrow, pyramidal tree with scale-like, evergreen needles. There are dozens of cultivars available, including shrubby dwarf varieties, varieties with yellow foliage and smaller upright varieties. (Zones 2–7; cultivars may be less cold hardy)

T. plicata (western arborvitae, western redcedar) is a narrowly pyramidal evergreen tree that grows quickly, resists deer browsing and maintains good foliage color all winter. Several cultivars are available, including several dwarf varieties and a yellow and green variegated variety. (Zones 5–9)

Also called: cedar **Features:** foliage; bark; form **Habit:** small to large, evergreen shrub or tree **Height:** 2–50' **Spread:** 2–20' **Hardiness:** zones 2–8

Ash
Fraxinus

A sh is not flashy, but it has many solid qualities. Its fall colors are gently glowing and luminous, a harmonious complement to the vivid oranges and reds of other autumn showoffs.

Growing

Ash grows best in **full sun**. The soil should be **fertile** and **moist** with a lot of room for root growth. These trees tolerate drought, poor soil, salt and pollution.

Tips

Ash is a quick-growing shade tree. It grows well in the moist soil alongside streams and ponds, or in low-lying areas that never seem to dry out.

Recommended

F. mandshurica (Manchurian ash) is more compact in form and very hardy. Seedless male clones are available

F. nigra (black ash, swamp ash) grows very tall and wide. Seedless cultivars are available that offer great fall color and longer periods in leaf.

F. pennsylvanica (green ash, red ash) is an irregular, spreading, tree. It grows very tall and equally as wide. Its foliage turns yellow, sometimes with orange or red, in fall. Seedless male clones are available.

Features: fall color; fast growth habit
Habit: upright or spreading, deciduous tree **Height:** 50–80' **Spread:** 25–80'
Hardiness: zones 3–8

F. pennsylvanica 'Variegata' (above)
F. pennsylvanica var. *subintegerrina* (below)

Ash is often planted in traffic medians and parking lots, and it will provide shade by the poolside.

Aspen
Populus

When you mention aspen or poplar, the response is often a scowl, based on a general dislike for the larger aspen varieties of old. The most popular varieties available today are vastly different from their cousins, which were considered messy and a nuisance.

Growing
Aspens prefer to grow in **full sun**. They are adaptable to any type of soil but prefer **deep soil** that is **rich**, **moist** and **well drained**.

Tips
The most popular aspens of late are the more recently introduced columnar varieties. Perfect for narrow or small spaces and for use as privacy screens, these clean, vigorous trees can be left as single specimens or planted in rows or groups for impact.

Recommended
P. tremula 'Erecta' (Swedish columnar aspen) is a seedless cultivar with a columnar growth habit. It is very popular because of its shallow and non-invasive root system, vigorous growth and overall form. Its narrow habit makes it ideal for privacy screening in newer housing developments where there's little space to waste or time to wait for growth.

P. tremuloides (quaking aspen) has rounded leaves that 'tremble' in the slightest breeze. This species forms thickets because of its underground root suckers.

P. tricocarpa (black cottonwood) is a large, vigorous tree that is native to Montana. It can grow quite tall and requires ample moisture.

P. tremula 'Erecta' (above & below)

Columnar trees can lend a formal touch to a flat landscape.

Also called: poplar, cottonwood **Features:** foliage; form; fast growth **Habit:** oval, columnar, deciduous tree **Flower color:** long, greenish catkins **Height:** 30–70' **Spread:** 5–10' **Hardiness:** zones 1–7

Barberry
Berberis

The variations available in plant size, foliage color and fruit make barberry a real workhorse of the plant world.

Growing

Barberry develops the best fall color when grown in **full sun**, but it tolerates partial shade. Any **well-drained** soil is suitable. This plant tolerates drought and urban conditions but suffers in poorly drained, wet soil.

Tips

Large barberry plants make great hedges with formidable prickles. Barberry can also be included in shrub and mixed borders. Small cultivars can be grown in rock gardens, in raised beds or along rock walls.

Recommended

B. koreana (Korean barberry) is a slightly larger species that has adapted to dry sites throughout the state. This is a very cold-hardy species.

B. thunbergii (Japanese barberry) is a dense shrub with a broad, rounded habit. The foliage is bright green and turns variable shades of orange, red or purple in fall. Yellow spring flowers are followed by glossy red fruit later in summer. Many cultivars have been developed for their variable foliage color, including shades of purple, yellow and variegated varieties.

Features: foliage; flowers; fruit **Habit:** prickly, deciduous shrub **Flower color:** yellow **Height:** 12"–5' **Spread:** $1^1/_2$–5' **Hardiness:** zones 4–8

B. thunbergii 'Crimson Pygmy' (above); *B. thunbergii* 'Atropupurea' (below)

Some regions have banned all Berberis *in the belief that all species are hosts for the destructive wheat rust fungus.* B. thunbergii *and several other species do not harbor this fungus, however.*

Birch
Betula

B. pendula 'Youngii' (above); B. papyrifera (below)

It seems as if birch trees have graced the Montana landscape forever. Although birch has struggled in times of drought, it has earned a respected status throughout the state.

Growing

Birches grow well in **full sun, partial shade** or **light shade**. The soil should be of **average to rich fertility, well drained** and **moist**. Many birch species naturally grow in wet areas, such as alongside streams. They don't, however, like permanently soggy conditions. Prune only in late summer or fall to prevent sap loss.

Tips

Often used as a specimen tree, the birch's small leaves and open canopy provide light shade that allows perennials, annuals or lawns to flourish beneath.

Recommended

B. papyrifera (paper birch, white birch) is native to parts of eastern Montana and is a staple in many residential settings. It has creamy white bark that peels off in layers, exposing cinnamon-colored bark beneath. Yellowish catkins dangle from the branches in early spring. This species is resistant to bronze birch borer. Cultivars with purple leaves or in a columnar form are also available.

B. pendula (weeping birch, European birch) has brown, papery bark that turns white with maturity. Cultivars that offer lacy leaves, smaller forms or weeping or columnar growth habits are also available.

Features: foliage; habit; bark; winter and early-spring catkins **Habit:** open, deciduous tree **Height:** 30–50' **Spread:** 20–30' **Hardiness:** zones 2–8

Black Locust
Robinia

Black locust is perhaps not the best choice for the front yard, but if you need a tough customer for a disturbed or recently flooded site, then black locust is the tree for you.

Growing
Black locust prefers **full sun**. It does best in **average to fertile, moist** soil but adapts to any soils that aren't constantly soggy. It tolerates infertile or salty soils, drought and pollution. Avoid growing this tree in exposed locations because heavy wind can cause the weak branches to break.

It is best to train black locust trees when they are young. Prune young trees to have a central leader and well-spaced branches. Remove suckers and branches that will form a narrow crotch. Large cuts on *Robinia* species do not heal well and should be avoided. Prune in late summer to avoid excessive bleeding.

Tips
Black locust is best used in difficult areas where other trees have failed to thrive. It can also be used in shelterbelts and as a firewood source.

All parts of this tree contain poisonous proteins. The bean-like seeds should never be eaten.

'Frisia'

Recommended
R. pseudoacacia is an upright, suckering and self-seeding, deciduous tree. It has deeply furrowed bark and produces dangling clusters of fragrant, white flowers in early summer. **'Frisia'** has golden yellow foliage that turns yellow-green in summer and orange-gold in fall. TWISTY BABY ('Lace Lady') is a small, often grafted selection with contorted and twisted branches. It produces few to no flowers. The twisted branches make a good winter garden feature.

This tree is in the bean or legume family. It is related to honeylocust, which has narrower leaflets.

Also called: false acacia **Features:** foliage; flowers; fast growth; spiny branches **Habit:** open, deciduous tree **Flower color:** white **Height:** 8–90' **Spread:** 10–40' **Hardiness:** zones 3–8

Buffaloberry
Shepherdia

S. argentea (above & below)

With its attractive appearance and drought-tolerant, easy-going nature, buffaloberry deserves to be more widely used. It has grown on the prairies for hundreds of years. Buffaloberry's red berries were once used to flavor buffalo meat, hence its name.

Growing

Buffaloberry grows best in **full sun**. The soil should be **well drained** and of **average fertility**.

Silver buffaloberry is best planted as a hedge or shelterbelt because of its mature size and suckering habit. This is particularly the case in eastern Montana.

Tips

Buffaloberry is the ideal shrub for informal borders, naturalization and shelterbelts.

Recommended

S. argentea (silver buffaloberry) is a large shrub with an aggressive growth habit. Narrow, silvery leaves are produced on thorny, twisted branches. Female plants produce yellow flowers followed by small red berries in fall. A cultivar of *S. argentea* that bears yellow fruit rather than red is available.

S. canadensis (russet buffaloberry) is a rounded, bushy shrub with dark greenish silver foliage that has brown scales on the undersides of the leaves. It bears tiny, inconspicuous, bright yellow flowers followed by red berries in fall.

Features: silvery foliage; vigorous growth habit **Habit:** large, bushy, upright, deciduous shrub **Height:** 3–16' **Spread:** 3' to indefinite **Hardiness:** zones 2–8

Caragana
Caragana

Caragana is hardy to zone 2, holds its own on dry, exposed sites and has the ability to fix nitrogen in the soil. When all other shrubs have succumbed to wicked conditions, caragana still thrives.

Growing

Caragana prefers **full sun** but tolerates partial or light shade. Soil of **average to high fertility** is preferred. This plant will adapt to just about any growing condition and tolerates dry, exposed locations, for example, in eastern Montana.

Tips

Caragana plants are grown as windbreaks and as formal or informal hedges. Caragana can be included in borders, and weeping forms are often used as specimen plants.

Recommended

C. arborescens is a large, twiggy, thorny shrub with upright or arching branches. Yellow, pea-like flowers are borne in late spring, followed by seedpods that ripen to brown in summer and rattle when blown by the wind. Grafted standards that resemble leafy umbrellas are available in various sizes, with either rounded or needle-like leaves.

C. frutex (Russian caragana) is a large shrub with few thorns, dark green foliage and bright yellow flowers.

C. pygmaea (pygmy caragana) is a compact, mounded shrub with finely textured foliage and lemon-colored flowers, followed by brown pod-like fruits.

Caraganas are almost impossible to kill. They have superior heat and drought tolerance but fail in locations that are too moist.

Also called: peashrub **Features:** late-spring flowers; foliage; habit **Habit:** prickly, grafted, weeping or upright, rounded shrub **Flower color:** yellow **Height:** 3–20' **Spread:** 8–18' **Hardiness:** zones 2–7

Cinquefoil
Potentilla (Pentaphylloides)

'Abbotswood' (above); *P. fruticosa* (below)

Cinquefoil is a fuss-free shrub that blooms madly all summer.

Growing
Cinquefoil prefers **full sun** but tolerates partial or light shade. Preferably the soil should be of **poor to average fertility** and **well drained**. This plant tolerates most conditions, including sandy or clay soil and wet or dry conditions. Established plants are drought tolerant. Too much fertilizer or too rich a soil will encourage weak, floppy, disease-prone growth.

Tips
Cinquefoil is useful in a shrub or mixed border. The smaller cultivars can be included in rock gardens and on rock walls. On steep slopes, potentilla can prevent soil erosion and reduce time spent maintaining the lawn. It can even be used to form a low, informal hedge.

If your cinquefoil's flowers fade in direct sun or hot weather, move the plant to a cooler location with some shade from the hot afternoon sun. Colors should revive in fall as the weather cools. Yellow-flowered plants are least likely to be affected by heat and sun.

Recommended
Of the many cultivars of *P. fruticosa* (*Pentaphylloides floribunda*), the following are a few of the most popular and interesting. **'Abbotswood'** is one of the best white-flowered cultivars, **'Pink Beauty'** bears pink, semi-double flowers, **'Tangerine'** has orange flowers and **'Yellow Gem'** has bright yellow flowers.

Also called: shrubby cinquefoil, potentilla, golden hardhack **Features:** flowers; foliage; habit **Habit:** mounding, deciduous shrub **Flower color:** white, pink, orange, yellow **Height:** 3–48" **Spread:** 12–36" **Hardiness:** zones 2–7

Cotoneaster

Cotoneaster

C. apiculatus (above); *C. acutifolius* (below)

With their diverse sizes, shapes, flowers, fruit and foliage, cotoneasters are so versatile that they border on being overused.

Growing

Cotoneasters grow well in **full sun** or **partial shade**. The soil should be of **average fertility** and **well drained**.

Tips

Cotoneasters can be included in shrub or mixed borders. Low spreaders work well as groundcover and shrubby species can be used to form hedges. Larger species are grown as small specimen trees and some low growers are grafted onto standards and grown as small, weeping trees.

Features: foliage; early-summer flowers; persistent fruit; variety of forms **Habit:** evergreen or deciduous groundcover, shrub or small tree **Flower color:** white **Height:** 1–10' **Spread:** 3–7' **Hardiness:** zones 3–8

Recommended

Many cotoneasters are available. *C. acutifolius* (Peking cotoneaster) is a frequently used hedging form. *C. adpressus* (creeping cotoneaster) is low-growing, and *C. apiculatus* (cranberry cotoneaster) is a low-spreading plant. *C. lucidus* (hedge cotoneaster) is also used for hedging because of its dense growth habit, dark lustrous leaves and great fall color. These are just a few possibilities; your local garden center will be able to help you find a suitable one for your garden.

Although cotoneaster berries are not poisonous, they can cause stomach upset if eaten in large quantities. The foliage may be toxic.

Currant
Ribes

R. alpinum (above & below)

Currant shrubs have proven highly useful to northern gardeners. Certain varieties are grown for their ornamental attributes, while others produce mouth-watering fruit that can be eaten right off the bush or used to make jellies, jams and pies.

Growing

Currant grows well in **full sun** or **partial shade.** The soil should be of **average fertility, moist, well drained** and **rich in organic matter.**

Tips

Currant can be used in a shrub or mixed border, on the edge of a garden bed or as a hedge. Alpine currant makes an excellent hedge.

Recommended

R. alpinum (alpine currant) is a dense, bushy, rounded shrub that tolerates shade and pollution. It bears yellow-green flowers in spring, followed by red berries on the female plants.

R. aureum (golden currant), a Montana native, is an upright shrub with slightly arching stems and blue-green foliage that turns red in fall. Fragrant, yellow flowers are borne in spring, followed by black berries.

R. sativum (red currant) is dense and vigorous, with edible red berries. It is native to western Montana.

Features: spring flowers; fruit; foliage **Habit:** upright, deciduous shrub with arching stems **Flower color:** yellow, yellow-green **Height:** 3–8' **Spread:** 3–8' **Hardiness:** zones 2–7

Dogwood
Cornus

Whether your garden is wet, dry, sunny or shaded, there is a dogwood for almost every condition. Stem color, leaf variegation, fall color, growth habit, soil adaptability and hardiness are all positive attributes to be found in the dogwoods.

Growing

Dogwoods grow equally well in **full sun, light shade** or **partial shade**, with a slight preference for light shade. The soil should be of **average to high fertility, high in organic matter, neutral or slightly acidic** and **well drained**.

Tips

Use shrub dogwoods along the edge of a woodland, in a shrub or mixed border, alongside a house, or near a pond, water feature or patio. They look best in groups rather than as single specimens.

Recommended

C. alba (red-twig dogwood, Tartarian dogwood) and *C. sericea* (*C. stolonifera*; red-osier dogwood) are native to Montana and grown for their bright red stems that provide winter interest. Cultivars are available with stems in varied shades of red, orange and yellow. Fall foliage color can also be attractive.

C. alba 'Siberian Pearl' (above); *C. sericea* (below)

Features: late-spring to early-summer flowers; fall foliage; stem color; fruit; habit **Habit:** deciduous, large shrub or small tree **Flower color:** white **Height:** 5–15' **Spread:** 5–20' **Hardiness:** zones 2–8

Douglas-Fir
Pseudotsuga

We are very lucky to have magnificent native trees like Douglas-firs. Not only can they be used as large specimens, but they also can be planted as seedlings in the smallest of gardens and then cut for use as Christmas trees in the future. The soft needles persist longer on cut trees than the needles of spruce and fir trees.

Growing
Douglas-fir prefers **full sun**. The soil should be of **average fertility, moist, acidic** and **well drained**. Pruning is generally not required.

Tips
Douglas-fir can be grown as a single large specimen tree or as part of a group of trees. Smaller cultivars can be grown as specimens in gardens or as part of shrub or mixed borders. The species is better adapted to western Montana and the foothills of central Montana.

Recommended
P. menziesii is a massive, native tree that can reach great age and height. Several less imposing cultivars of Douglas-fir work well in small gardens.

Douglas-fir cones have unique three-pronged bracts that look like the hind feet and tails of tiny mice hiding inside.

Features: foliage; cones; habit
Habit: conical evergreen, becomes columnar with age **Height:** 6–200'
Spread: 6–25' **Hardiness:** zones 4–7

Elderberry

Sambucus

S. racemosa (above & below)

Elderberries work well in a natural-ized garden. Cultivars are available that will provide light texture in a dark area, dark foliage in a bright area, or variegated yellow foliage and bright stems in brilliant sunshine.

Growing
Elderberries grow well in **full sun** or **partial shade**. Cultivars and varieties grown for interesting leaf color develop the best color in light or partial shade. The soil should be of **average fertility, moist** and **well drained**. These plants tolerate dry soil once established.

Tips
Elderberries can be used in a shrub or mixed border, in a natural woodland garden, or next to a pond or other water feature. Types with interesting or colorful foliage can be used as specimen plants or focal points in the garden.

Recommended
S. canadensis (American elder/elderberry) and **S. racemosa** (European red elder/elderberry) are rounded shrubs with white or pinkish white flowers followed by red or dark purple berries. Cultivars are available with green, yellow, bronze or purple foliage and deeply divided feathery foliage. Both species are found growing wild in parts of the state.

Features: early-summer flowers; fruit; foliage **Habit:** large, bushy, deciduous shrub **Flower color:** white, pink **Height:** 5–10' **Spread:** 5–10' **Hardiness:** zones 3–9

Elm

Ulmus

U. americana 'New Harmony' (above); U. americana (below)

DED is a realistic threat, but it can be prevented if you know what to look for. Learn everything you possibly can about DED to protect our elms.

Elms are stately trees that are often used in public spaces for their statuesque appearance and wide appeal.

Growing

Elms grow well in **full sun** or **partial shade**. They adapt to most soil conditions but prefer a **moist, fertile** soil. Prune out all dead wood that provides beetle habitat. Prune live wood only during the winter months.

Tips

The smaller species and cultivars of elms make attractive specimen and shade trees, while larger trees look attractive on larger properties and in parks, where they have plenty of room to grow.

Recommended

U. americana (American elm) is a vase-shaped tree with arching branches. It grows very tall and wide. Consider cultivars that are more resistant to Dutch elm disease (DED), such as the Alberta-bred Brandon elm and the Liberty elm. The species is another native to eastern Montana.

U. pumila (Siberian elm, dwarf elm) is a medium-sized, vase-shaped tree with a high level of drought and disease tolerance. The cultivars are far more desirable, with stronger branches, better winter hardiness and overall appeal. Consult your local garden center to get cultivar recommendations.

Features: form; fall color; inconspicuous flowers; habit **Habit:** vase-shaped, open, deciduous tree **Height:** 55–110' **Spread:** 35–60' **Hardiness:** zones 2–8

Euonymus
Euonymus

Euonymus makes a fine specimen and works well as a background or border plant for stunning fall color and interesting bark. The wintercreeper euonymus, with its interesting leaf colorings and plant habits, also has many uses.

Growing

Euonymus species prefer **full sun** and tolerate light or partial shade. Soil of **average to rich fertility** is preferable but any **moist, well-drained** soil will do.

Tips

E. alatus can be grown in a shrub or mixed border, as a specimen, in a naturalistic garden or as a hedge. Dwarf cultivars can be used to create informal hedges. *E. fortunei* can be grown as a shrub in borders or as a hedge. It is an excellent substitute for the more demanding boxwood. The trailing habit also makes it useful as a groundcover or climber.

Recommended

E. alatus (burning bush, winged euonymus) is an attractive, open, mounding, deciduous shrub with vivid red fall foliage. Winter interest is provided by the corky ridges, or wings, that grow on the stems and branches. Cultivars are available. (Zones 3–8)

E. fortunei (wintercreeper euonymus) as a species is rarely grown owing to the wide and attractive variety of cultivars. These can be prostrate, climbing

E. alatus 'Cole's Select' (above); *E. fortunei* cultivar (below)

or mounding evergreens, often with attractive, variegated foliage. Winter protection is necessary. (Zones 4–8)

E. nana **var. *turkestanica*** (Turkestan burning bush) is a sprawling shrub with a rounded, upright habit. It produces fine textured foliage and showy pink and orange pendent flowers. Good fall color.

Features: foliage; corky stems (*E. alatus*); habit **Habit:** deciduous and evergreen shrub, small tree, groundcover or climber **Flower color:** pink, orange **Height:** 1–6' **Spread:** 2–6' **Hardiness:** zones 2–8

Fir

Abies

Many people aren't aware that there are a number of hardy and beautiful fir varieties available that will thrive in Montana. The trees are stately in appearance and the compact shrub varieties are ideal for rock gardens and small yards.

Growing

Firs usually prefer **full sun** but tolerate partial shade. The soil should be **rich, moist, neutral to acidic** and **well drained.** Firs prefer a **sheltered** site out of the wind, and they generally will not tolerate polluted city conditions. *A. concolor* tolerates pollution, heat and drought better than other *Abies* species.

Tips

Firs make impressive specimen trees in large areas. Dwarf cultivars can be included in shrub borders or planted as specimens.

Recommended

A. balsamea (balsam fir) looks pyramidal when it's young but narrows as it ages. (Zones 3–6)

A. concolor (white fir) is a large, pyramidal to conic tree. The needles have a whitish coating that gives the tree a hazy blue appearance. Cultivars with even whiter needles are also available.

A. lasiocarpa (subalpine fir) is a narrow, pyramidal tree that grows large in moist, sheltered locations. (Zones 3–8)

A. concolor 'Candicans' (above & below)

A. balsamea *occurs naturally from northern Alberta to Labrador and southward to Pennsylvania. This is the largest geographical distribution of any North American fir species.*

Features: foliage; cones **Habit:** narrow, pyramidal or columnar evergreen tree **Height:** 2–70' **Spread:** 3–25' **Hardiness:** zones 3–7

Flowering Cherry, Plum, Almond & Chokecherry

Prunus

Cherries and plums are so beautiful and uplifting after the gray days of winter that few gardeners can resist them.

Growing

These flowering fruit trees prefer **full sun**. The soil should be of **average fertility, moist** and **well drained**. Shallow roots will emerge from the lawn if the tree is not getting sufficient water.

Tips

Tree and shrub species are beautiful as specimen plants and many are small enough for most gardens. Small species and cultivars can be included in borders or grouped to form informal hedges or barriers. Double-flowering plum, Nanking cherry and purpleleaf sand cherry can be trained into informal hedges.

Recommended

P. besseyi (western sand cherry) is frequently used as a shrubby pollinator for plums, and it bears glossy green foliage and white flowers. *P.* x *cistena* (purpleleaf sand cherry) is a shrub grown for its purple foliage and light pink flowers. *P. fruticosa* (Mongolian cherry) bears tasty, sour cherries ideal for preserves and pies. *P. tomentosa* (Nanking cherry) is a rounded, blooming shrub with tart, red berries.

A great number of tree varieties are popular throughout Montana. *P. mackii* (amur cherry) is a small, rounded tree

P. virginiana 'Schubert' (above); P. tomentosa (below)

with attractive bark. *P. padus* (Mayday) bears pink or white blossoms in early spring. *P. pensylvanica* (pin cherry) produces sour cherries on a small, slender, often shrubby tree. *P. virginiana* (chokecherry) is a medium-sized tree, with tiny, white flowers and fruit adored by birds. Some of the cultivars bear dark, burgundy foliage.

Features: spring to early-summer flowers; fruit; bark; fall foliage **Habit:** upright, rounded, spreading or weeping, deciduous tree or shrub **Flower color:** white, pink **Height:** 3–35' **Spread:** 3–30' **Hardiness:** zones 2–8

Forsythia
Forsythia

F. x intermedia (above & below)

Correct pruning after flowering is finished will keep forsythias looking attractive. Flowers are produced on growth that is one year old. On mature plants, cut one-third of the oldest growth back to the ground each year.

Forsythia's bright, lemon yellow flowers are indicators of warmer days ahead. While other plants have yet to wake from their deep winter sleep, forsythia blooms like crazy. Copious amounts of leaves follow the flowers throughout the warm summer months.

Growing
Forsythias grow best in **full sun** but tolerate light shade. The soil should be of **average fertility**, **moist** and **well drained**.

Tips
These shrubs look gorgeous in flower. Plant one in a shrub or mixed border where other flowering plants can take over once the forsythia's early blooming season has passed. Forsythia are better adapted to warm, protected areas of western Montana.

Recommended
F. x **intermedia** (border forsythia) is a large shrub with upright stems that arch as they mature. Yellow flowers emerge before the leaves in early to mid-spring. Many cultivars have been developed from this hybrid. (This species is hardy to zone 4 but the flowerbuds may be killed in zones 5 and colder.) Flowering can be sporadic, depending on exposure. A sheltered location is best.

F. ovata (early forsythia) is an upright, spreading shrub that bears bright yellow, pendent flowers in early spring, followed by dense tufts of smooth foliage. A number of cultivars are available. (Zones 4–8)

Features: early-spring blooming; dense growth habit **Habit:** bushy, deciduous, upright shrub **Flower color:** yellow **Height:** 6' **Spread:** 6' **Hardiness:** zones 3–8

Hackberry
Celtis

Although hackberry isn't a top-ten seller in Montana yet, it should be. It tolerates most conditions in our state, and it responds with brawn and grace.

Growing
Hackberry prefers **full sun**. It adapts to a variety of soil types including poor and dry soils. **Deep soils** with **adequate moisture** and **drainage** are best.

Tips
Hackberry is an ideal shade tree specimen for expansive, windy areas. It grows as tall as it does wide and requires a lot of space to reach its full size without conflict.

Recommended
C. occidentalis is a medium to large tree with a rounded head. The head is made up of arching branches covered in simple but classic foliage. Inconspicuous flowers emerge in spring followed by dark red or purple pea-sized fruits in fall.

C. occidentalis (above & below)

Hackberry is related to the American elm but is completely immune to Dutch elm disease.

Also called: American hackberry, common hackberry **Features:** form; hardiness; colorful berries; inconspicuous flowers; tolerance to poor conditions **Habit:** high-headed, oval, deciduous tree **Height:** 30–50' **Spread:** 30–50' **Hardiness:** zones 2–8

Hawthorn

Crataegus

C. laevigata (above); C. laevigata 'Paul's Scarlet' (below)

Hawthorns are uncommonly beautiful trees, with a generous spring show of beautiful, miniature, rose-like blossoms, persistent glossy red fruit and good fall color.

Growing

Hawthorns grow equally well in **full sun** or **partial shade**. They adapt to any **well-drained** soil and tolerate urban conditions.

Tips

Hawthorns can be grown as specimen plants for informal landscapes and gardens. They require little care and are the ideal flowering ornamentals for small spaces.

These trees are small enough to include in most gardens. However, with their stiff, 2" long, sharp thorns, hawthorns might not be a good selection if there are children about.

Recommended

C. douglasii (black hawthorn) is a medium-sized, thorny, low-headed tree with gray bark and reddish twigs. It bears clusters of white flowers followed by black fruit. Cultivars are available and are grown more frequently than the species.

C. laevigata (*C. oxycantha*; English hawthorn) is a low-branching, rounded tree with zigzag layers of thorny branches. It bears white or pink flowers followed by red fruit in late summer. Many cultivars are available. (Zones 4–8)

C. x *mordenensis* is a small, ornamental tree, bearing double, white or pink flowers followed by sparse red berries. A few cultivars are available.

Features: late-spring or early-summer flowers; fruit; foliage; thorny branches **Habit:** rounded, deciduous tree, often with a zigzag, layered branch pattern and twisted trunk **Flower color:** white, pink **Height:** 15–30' **Spread:** 10–20' **Hardiness:** zones 3–8

Hemlock

Tsuga

T. canadensis 'Jeddeloh' (above); *T. canadensis* (below)

Many people would agree that eastern hemlock is one of the most beautiful, graceful evergreen trees in the world. Its movement, grace and soft appearance make it easy to place in the landscape.

Growing

Hemlock generally grows well in any light from **full sun to full shade**. The soil should be **humus rich, moist** and **well drained**. Hemlock is drought sensitive and grows best in cool, moist conditions. It is also sensitive to air pollution and suffers salt damage, so keep it away from roadways.

Features: foliage; habit; cones **Habit:** pyramidal or columnar, evergreen tree or shrub **Height:** 18"–80' **Spread:** 18"–35' **Hardiness:** zones 3–8

Tips

This elegant tree, with its delicate needles, is one of the most beautiful evergreens to use as a specimen tree in western Montana. Hemlock can be pruned to keep it within bounds or shaped to form a hedge. The many dwarf forms are useful in smaller gardens.

Recommended

T. canadensis (eastern hemlock, Canadian hemlock) is a graceful, narrowly pyramidal tree. Many cultivars are available, including groundcover and pendulous and dwarf forms.

Honeylocust

Gleditsia

G. triacanthos var. inermis (above & below)

This adaptable, quick-growing tree provides very light shade, making it a good choice for lawns.

Thornless honeylocust remains a popular tree for lawn and street plantings. The brilliant, deep yellow fall color is wonderful to behold.

Growing

Thornless honeylocust prefers **full sun**. The soil should be **fertile** and **well drained**. This tree adapts to most soil types.

Tips

Use thornless honeylocust and its numerous cultivars as street trees or specimen trees in larger yards in the warmer parts of Montana. Smaller selections are more appropriate for smaller yards.

Recommended

G. triacanthos var. *inermis* is a spreading, rounded to flat-topped, thornless tree with inconspicuous flowers and sometimes long, pea-like pods that persist into fall. The fall color is a warm, golden yellow.

Many cultivars are available, including compact and weeping varieties, and varieties with bright yellow, spring foliage.

Features: summer and fall foliage; habit
Habit: rounded, spreading, deciduous tree
Height: 15–100' **Spread:** 15–70'
Hardiness: zones 4–8

Honeysuckle

Lonicera

L. tatarica (above & below)

Honeysuckle produces beautiful, exotic flowers on both its shrub and vine varieties. It's easy to care for and offers a little tropical flare in late spring.

Growing

Honeysuckles grow well in **full sun** or **partial shade**. The soil should be **average to fertile** and **well drained**. Climbing honeysuckles prefer a **moist, humus-rich** soil.

Tips

Shrubby honeysuckles can be used in mixed borders, in naturalized gardens and as hedges. Most are large and take up a lot of space when mature. A climbing honeysuckle can be trained to grow up a trellis, fence, arbor or other structure.

Recommended

L. tatarica (tatarian honeysuckle) is a large, bushy, deciduous shrub that grows very tall with an equal spread. It bears pink, white or red flowers in late spring and early summer. Varieties and cultivars are available in varied forms, sizes and flower colors.

Honeysuckle flowers are often scented and attract hummingbirds, bees and other pollinating insects.

Features: flowers; habit; fruit **Habit:** rounded, upright shrub or twining climber **Flower color:** pink, white, red **Height:** 10–12' **Spread:** 10' **Hardiness:** zones 3–8

Hydrangea
Hydrangea

ydrangeas have many attractive qualities, including showy, often long-lasting flowers and glossy green leaves, some of which turn beautiful colors in fall.

Growing

Hydrangeas grow well in **full sun** or **partial shade**, and some species tolerate full shade. Shade or partial shade will reduce leaf and flower scorch in hotter gardens. The soil should be of **average to high fertility, humus rich, moist** and **well drained**. These plants do best in cool, moist conditions.

Tips

Hydrangeas come in many forms and have many uses in the landscape. They can be included in shrub or mixed borders, used as specimens or informal barriers and planted in groups or containers.

Recommended

H. arborescens (smooth hydrangea) is a rounded shrub that flowers well, even in shady conditions. This species is rarely grown in favor of the cultivars that bear large clusters of showy white blossoms.

H. paniculata (panicle hydrangea) is a spreading to upright large shrub or small tree that bears white flowers from late summer to early fall. **'Grandiflora'** (Peegee hydrangea) is a commonly available cultivar.

H. paniculata 'Grandiflora' (above); *H. paniculata* (below)

Features: flowers; foliage; bark; habit
Habit: deciduous, mounding or spreading shrub or tree **Flower color:** white **Height:** 36" **Spread:** 36" **Hardiness:** zones 3–8

Juniper
Juniperus

With the wide variety of junipers available, from low-creeping plants to upright pyramidal forms, there are endless uses for them in the garden.

Growing
Junipers prefer **full sun** but tolerate light shade. Ideally the soil should be of **average fertility** and **well drained**, but these plants tolerate most conditions.

Tips
Junipers can make prickly barriers and hedges, and they can be used in borders, as specimens or in groups. The larger species can be used to form windbreaks, while the low-growing species can be used in rock gardens and as groundcovers.

Recommended
Junipers vary from species to species and often within a species. Cultivars are available for all species and may differ significantly from the species. *J. chinensis* (Chinese juniper) is a conical tree or spreading shrub. *J. communis* (common juniper) is a low-growing, spreading species. *J. horizontalis* (creeping juniper) is a prostrate, creeping groundcover. *J. sabina* (savin juniper) is a low-growing, groundcover species. *J. scopulorum* (Rocky Mountain juniper) can be upright, rounded, weeping or spreading. *J. squamata* (singleseed juniper) forms a prostrate or low-spreading shrub, or a small, upright tree.

J. chinensis 'Spartan' (above)
J. horizontalis 'Blue Prince' (below)

Wear long sleeves and gloves when handling junipers—the prickly foliage gives some gardeners a rash. Juniper 'berries' are poisonous if eaten in large quantities.

Features: foliage; variety of color; size; habit **Habit:** conical or columnar tree; rounded or spreading shrub; prostrate groundcover; evergreen **Height:** 4"–16' **Spread:** 2–8' **Hardiness:** zones 2–8

Larch
Larix

L. decidua 'Pendula' (above); L. decidua (below)

Larch makes an interesting specimen tree. It is one of the few needled trees that loses its foliage each year.

Growing
Larch grows best in **full sun**. The soil should be of **average fertility**, **acidic**, **moist** and **well drained**. Although tolerant of most conditions, this tree doesn't like dry or chalky soils.

Tips
This deciduous conifer likes cool, wet sites. It detests heat and drought, so careful placement is necessary.

Recommended
L. decidua (European larch) is a large, narrow, pyramidal tree with soft, green needles that turn bronzy yellow in fall. A weeping cultivar and a tall, conical variety exist as well.

L. occidentalis (western larch) is a large, pyramidal tree native to western Montana. It can grow up to 150' tall with a 30' spread.

L. siberica (Siberian larch) is a more densely leaved species compared to other species. It is a medium-sized tree that is very cold hardy and tolerant to drought.

Larches are good trees for attracting birds to the garden. The size of the low, weeping cultivars suits most residential gardens.

Features: summer and fall foliage; habit **Habit:** pyramidal, deciduous conifer **Height:** 45–150' **Spread:** 25–30' **Hardiness:** zones 1–7

Lilac

Syringa

There is no end to the colors, sizes, shapes and scents of lilacs available. A Montana garden would be incomplete without at least one lilac.

Growing

Lilacs grow best in **full sun**. The soil should be **fertile, humus rich** and **well drained**. These plants tolerate open, windy locations.

Tips

Include lilacs in a shrub or mixed border or use them to create an informal hedge. Japanese tree lilac can be used as a specimen tree.

Recommended

S. x *chinensis* (Chinese lilac) is a rounded shrub with arching branches and double, purple flowers. Cultivars and varieties are available. (Zones 4–8)

S. x *hyacinthiflora* (hyacinth-flowered lilac, early-flowering lilac) is a hardy, upright hybrid that becomes spreading as it matures. Clusters of fragrant flowers appear two weeks earlier than the French lilac. The leaves turn reddish purple in fall. (Zones 3–7)

S. meyeri (Meyer lilac) is a compact, rounded shrub that bears fragrant pink or lavender flowers. (Zones 3–7)

S. patula (Manchurian lilac) is an upright, vigorous shrub that offers cultivars in compact forms. (Zones 3–8)

S. x *prestoniae* (Preston lilac) is an extremely hardy, dense, mounding shrub with crinkly foliage. It blooms

S. *vulgaris* 'Sensation' (above); S. *vulgaris* (below)

approximately two weeks later than the French lilac.

S. villosa (villosa or late lilac) blooms later than other lilacs. It produces cream-colored to pink flowers and does not sucker like *S. vulgaris*.

S. vulgaris (French lilac, common lilac) is the shrub most people think of when they think of lilacs. It is a suckering, spreading shrub with an irregular habit that bears fragrant, lilac-colored flowers. (Zones 3–8)

Features: late-spring to mid-summer flowers; habit **Habit:** rounded, deciduous shrub or small tree **Flower color:** cream, pink, lilac, lavender, purple **Height:** 4–25' **Spread:** 4–20' **Hardiness:** zones 2–8

Linden
Tilia

T. mongolica 'Harvest Gold' (above)

Lindens are picturesque shade trees with a signature gumdrop shape and sweet-scented flowers that capture the essence of summer.

Growing
Lindens grow best in **full sun**. The soil should be **average to fertile, moist** and **well drained**. These trees adapt to most pH levels but prefer an **alkaline** soil. They tolerate urban conditions and pollution.

Tips
Lindens are useful and attractive street, shade and specimen trees. Their tolerance of pollution and their moderate size make lindens ideal for city gardens.

Recommended
T. americana (American linden, basswood) is a large tree with heart-shaped leaves and fragrant, yellow flowers. Cultivars are available.

T. cordata (littleleaf linden) is a dense, pyramidal tree that may become rounded with age. It bears small, fragrant flowers with narrow, yellow-green bracts. Cultivars are available.

T. mongolica (Mongolian linden) is an upright, round-headed tree with exfoliating bark and spectacular fall color. Cultivars are available.

Features: foliage; flowers; habit **Habit:** dense, pyramidal to rounded, deciduous tree **Flower color:** yellow **Height:** 30–45' **Spread:** 20–35' **Hardiness:** zones 3–8

Maple
Acer

$\mathcal{M}$ aples are beautiful all year, with attractive foliage and hanging samaras in summer, vibrant leaf color in fall and interesting bark and branch structures in winter.

Growing

Generally, maples do well in **full sun** or **light shade,** though this varies from species to species. The soil should be **fertile, moist, high in organic matter** and **well drained**.

Tips

Maples can be used as specimen trees, as large elements in shrub or mixed borders or as hedges. Some are useful as understory plants bordering wooded areas; others can be grown in containers on patios or terraces. Few Japanese gardens are without the attractive smaller maples.

Recommended

Maples are some of the most stunning trees available. Many are very large when fully mature, but there are also a few smaller species that are useful in smaller gardens. There are far more hardy maples available than most people are aware of, so check with your local nursery or garden center for their recommendations.

A. platanoides 'Crimson King' (above); *A. p.* 'Drummondii' (below)

Features: foliage; bark; winged fruit; fall color; form **Habit:** small, multi-stemmed, deciduous tree or large shrub **Height:** 4–60' **Spread:** 4–45' **Hardiness:** zones 2–8

Mock-Orange
Philadelphus

P. coronarius 'Minnesota Snowflake' (above); *P. coronarius* (below)

Grow mock-orange if only for its heavenly fragrance, which is reminiscent of orange blossoms.

Growing

Mock-oranges grow well in **full sun**, **partial shade** or **light shade**. The soil should be of **average fertility**, **humus rich**, **moist** and **well drained**.

Tips

Include mock-oranges in shrub or mixed borders. Use them in groups to create barriers and screens.

Recommended

P. coronarius (sweet mock-orange) is an upright, broadly rounded shrub with fragrant, white flowers. It grows quite tall and wide. Cultivars with variegated or chartreuse foliage are available.

P. lewisii is a smaller, native shrub with white, citrus-scented, single flowers that float atop dark green, contrasting foliage. A wide variety of cultivars that offer double flowers and differing heights and spreads are available.

P. x *virginalis* (virginal mock orange) is an upright, medium-sized shrub. It bears single or double white flowers later than *P. coronarius*. Cultivars are available with large, double flowers.

Features: early-summer, fragrant flowers
Habit: rounded, deciduous shrub with arching branches **Flower color:** white **Height:** $1^{1}/_{2}$–12'
Spread: $1^{1}/_{2}$–12' **Hardiness:** zones 3–8

Mountain Ash

Sorbus

S. aucuparia (above)

Mountain ash is grown for its attractive, oval form, spring display of white flowers and red, orange or yellow fall fruit that persists into winter. The berries provide important forage for birds and are a visual feast.

Growing

Mountain ash grows well in **full sun**, **partial shade** or **light shade** in **average to fertile**, **humus-rich**, **well-drained** soil.

Tips

Commonly grown as a specimen tree, mountain ash is also ideal in woodland and natural settings where it attracts a variety of wildlife to the garden.

Recommended

S. aucuparia (European mountain ash) grows slightly taller than *S. americana* and bears large flower clusters, followed by orange-red berries in fall. Some of the most popular columnar cultivars are related to this species.

S. decora (showy mountain ash) is much shorter and half the width of the more traditional species. *S. decora*'s blooming cycle exceeds that of its relatives; it is more resistant to fireblight and it displays magnificent fall color.

S. x *hybrida* (oakleaf mountain ash) is a broad, upright tree. It produces dark leaves with downy white undersides that resemble oak leaves.

Mountain ash trees are available with either a single or multi-stemmed trunk.

Features: fall color; flowers; brightly colored, persistent fruit **Habit:** rounded or oval, deciduous tree **Flower color:** white **Height:** 16–40' **Spread:** 6–25' **Hardiness:** zones 2–7

Ninebark

Physocarpus

P. opulifolius DIABLO (above & below)

This North American native deserves wider recognition, especially now that attractive cultivars, with foliage ranging in color from yellow to purple, are available.

Growing

Ninebark grows well in **full sun** or **partial shade**. The best leaf coloring develops in a sunny location. The soil should be **fertile, acidic, moist** and **well drained**.

Tips

Ninebark can be included in a shrub or mixed border, in a woodland garden or in a wild garden.

Recommended

P. opulifolius (common ninebark) is a shrub with long, arching branches and exfoliating bark. It bears light pink or white flowers in early summer and fruit that ripens to reddish green or red in late fall. Several cultivars are available.

You may not actually find nine layers, but the peeling, flecked bark of ninebark does add interest to the winter landscape.

Also called: common ninebark **Features:** early-summer flowers; fruit; bark; foliage **Habit:** upright, sometimes suckering, deciduous shrub **Flower color:** pink, white **Height:** 5–8' **Spread:** 5–8' **Hardiness:** zones 2–8

Oak

Quercus

The oak's classic shape, outstanding fall color, deep roots and long life are some of its many assets. Plant it for its individual beauty and for posterity.

Growing

Oaks grow well in **full sun** or **partial shade**. The soil should be **fertile, moist** and **well drained**. These trees can be difficult to establish; transplant them only when they are young.

Tips

Oaks are large trees that are best as specimens or for spacious yards and gardens and public spaces. Do not disturb the ground around the base of an oak; this tree is very sensitive to changes in grade.

Recommended

The following are two popular oak species. **Q. macrocarpa** (bur or mossycup oak) is a stately, medium-sized tree with an open and upright habit, an oval crown, very large and deeply lobed leaves and bark that is deeply textured and corky in appearance. This is the only oak species native to Montana. **Q. rubra** (red oak) is a rounded, spreading tree with fall color ranging from yellow to red-brown. A variety of cultivars is available for each species; check with your local nursery or garden center.

Q. macrocarpa (above)

Acorns are generally not edible. Acorns of certain oak species are edible but usually must be processed first to leach out the bitter tannins.

Features: summer and fall foliage; bark; habit; acorns **Habit:** large, rounded, spreading, deciduous tree **Height:** 50–80' **Spread:** 25–50' **Hardiness:** zones 3–8

Ohio Buckeye
Aesculus

A. glabra (both photos)

Ohio buckeye is a hardy specimen with admirable qualities ideal for the prairie landscape. Its relatives are equally as beautiful and deserving of more frequent use.

Growing
Ohio buckeyes grow well in **full sun** or **partial shade**. The soil should be **fertile, moist** and **well drained**. These trees dislike excessive drought.

Tips
Ohio buckeyes are used as specimen and shade trees, but the roots can break up

These trees give heavy shade, which is excellent for cooling buildings, but can make it difficult to grow grass beneath them.

sidewalks and patios if planted too close to them.

The smaller, shrubby specimens grow well near pond plantings and also make interesting specimens. Give them plenty of space as they can form large colonies.

Recommended
A. glabra (Ohio buckeye) is an extremely hardy tree that produces masses of green-yellow flowers that emerge from each branch tip in early summer. The ornate foliage turns brilliant yellow in fall.

Features: early-summer flowers; foliage; spiny fruit **Habit:** rounded or spreading deciduous tree or shrub **Flower color:** green-yellow **Height:** 25–35' **Spread:** 20–30' **Hardiness:** zones 3–8

Ornamental Crabapple

Malus

Pure white to deep pink flowers, heights between 5' and 25' with similar spreads, tolerance of winter's extreme cold and summer's baking heat, plus tiny fruit—from green to candy apple red—that persists through winter. What more could anyone ask from a tree?

Growing

Crabapples prefer **full sun** but tolerate partial shade. The soil should be of **average to rich fertility, moist** and **well drained**. These trees tolerate damp soil.

To prevent the spread of crabapple pests and diseases, clean up all the leaves and fruit that fall from the tree. Many pests overwinter in the fruit, leaves or soil at the base of the tree. Clearing away their winter shelter helps keep populations under control.

Tips

Crabapples make excellent specimen plants. Many varieties are quite small, so there is one to suit almost any size of garden. Crabapples' flexible young branches make them good choices for creating espalier specimens along a wall or fence.

Recommended

There are hundreds of ornamental crabapples available. When choosing a species, variety or cultivar, the most important attributes to look for are disease resistance and size at maturity. Ask for information about new, resistant cultivars at your local nursery or garden center.

Features: spring flowers; late-season and winter fruit; fall foliage; habit; bark **Habit:** rounded, mounded or spreading, small to medium, deciduous tree **Flower color:** white, pink **Height:** 5–25' **Spread:** 6–20' **Hardiness:** zones 2–8

Pine
Pinus

P. *ponderosa* (above); P. *strobus* (below)

Pine varieties generally thrive in our climate; however, some pine species and cultivars are susceptible to both windburn and sunscorch. Consult your local garden center for recommendations.

Pines offer exciting possibilities for any garden. Exotic-looking pines are available with soft or stiff, silvery blue or gray needles; elegant, drooping branches; and flaky, copper-colored bark.

Growing
Pines grow best in **full sun**. These trees adapt to most **well-drained** soils but do not tolerate polluted urban conditions.

Tips
Pines can be used as specimen trees, as hedges or to create windbreaks. Smaller cultivars can be included in shrub or mixed borders. These trees are not heavy feeders; fertilizing will encourage rapid new growth that is weak and susceptible to pest and disease problems.

Recommended
There are many available pines, both trees and shrubby dwarf plants. Check with your local garden center or nursery to find out what is available.

Features: foliage; bark; cones, habit **Habit:** upright, columnar or spreading, evergreen tree
Height: 3–65' **Spread:** 3–25'
Hardiness: zones 2–8

Serviceberry
Amelanchier

The *Amelanchier* species are first-rate North American natives, bearing lacy, white flowers in spring, followed by edible berries. In fall, the foliage color ranges from glowing apricot to deep red.

Growing
Serviceberries grow well in **full sun** or **light shade**. They prefer **acidic soil** that is **fertile, humus rich, moist** and **well drained**. They do adjust to drought.

Tips
With spring flowers, edible fruit, attractive leaves that turn red in fall and often artistic branch growth, serviceberries make beautiful specimen plants or even shade trees in small gardens. The shrubbier forms can be grown along the edges of a woodland or in a border. In the wild these trees are often found growing near water sources and are beautiful beside ponds or streams.

Recommended
Several species and hybrids are available. **A. alnifolia** (serviceberry, Saskatoon, Juneberry) is a native shrub that has white flowers and edible blue-black fruit. **Var. semi-integrifolia** (*A. florida;* Pacific serviceberry) is a tall, upright shrub with white flowers followed by purplish black fruit. **A. canadensis** (shadblow serviceberry) is a large, upright, suckering shrub with white flowers and purple fruit. All of these shrubs have good fall color.

A. canadensis (above)

Serviceberry fruit can be used in place of blueberries in any recipe; the fruit has a similar, but generally sweeter, flavor.

Also called: saskatoon, juneberry **Features:** spring or early-summer flowers; edible fruit; fall color; habit; bark **Habit:** single- or multi-stemmed, deciduous, large shrub or small tree **Flower color:** white **Height:** 15–25' **Spread:** 15–20' **Hardiness:** zones 3–8

Snowberry
Symphoricarpos

S. *albus* (above & below)

These low-maintenance shrubs spread readily and fill in gaps in shady areas.

Snowberry is an excellent choice for naturalizing over large areas, and though its bloom is not spectacular, the bluish green foliage and white fruit are summer standouts.

Growing
Snowberry grows well in **full sun** or **partial or light shade**. This plant adapts to any soil that is **fertile** and **well drained**, and it can handle pollution, drought and exposure.

Tips
Snowberries can be used in shrub or mixed borders, as screens or informal hedges. They are great for use on hillsides, as their suckering roots bind the soil.

Recommended
S. albus is a rounded, suckering shrub with arching branches. The small, delicate, pinkish white summer flowers are rather inconspicuous but still attractive. The clusters of white berries that follow are interesting and persist through fall and early winter. Cultivars are available with variegated foliage and large fruit.

S. orbiculatus (buckbrush, coralberry, Indian currant) is a small shrub with a spreading habit. It bears dull green foliage and white flowers that have a reddish tinge. The flowers are followed by purplish red fruit. Cultivars are available.

Features: foliage; fall and winter fruit; habit **Habit:** rounded or spreading, deciduous shrub **Height:** 3–6' **Spread:** 3–6' **Hardiness:** zones 3–7

Spirea
Spiraea

S. x bumalda cultivar (above); *S. x vanhouttei* (below)

Spireas, seen in so many gardens and with dozens of cultivars, remain undeniable favorites. With a wide range of forms, sizes and colors of both foliage and flowers, spireas have many possible uses in the landscape.

Growing
Spireas prefer **full sun**. To help prevent foliage burn, provide protection from very hot sun. The soil should be **fertile, neutral to acidic, moist** and **well drained**.

Tips
Spireas are used in shrub or mixed borders, in rock gardens and as informal screens and hedges.

Recommended
Two popular hybrid groups of the many species and cultivars follow. **S. x *bumalda*** (*S. japonica* '**Bumalda**') is a low, broad, mounded shrub with pink flowers. It is rarely grown in favor of the many cultivars, which also have pink flowers but with brightly colored foliage. **S. x *vanhouttei*** (bridal wreath spirea, Vanhoutte spirea) is a dense, bushy shrub with arching branches that bears clusters of white flowers. Check your local nursery or garden center for additional varieties.

Features: summer flowers; habit **Habit:** round, bushy, deciduous shrub **Flower color:** white, pink **Height:** 3–8' **Spread:** 3–8' **Hardiness:** zones 3–8

Spruce
Picea

P. abies 'Nidiformis' (above); *P. pungens* var. *glauca* 'Moerheim' (below)

Spruce tree and shrub specimens are some of the most commonly grown evergreens throughout the state. Grow spruce where they have enough room to spread, then let them branch all the way to the ground.

Growing
Spruce trees grow best in **full sun**. The soil should be **deep, moist, well drained** and **neutral to acidic**. These trees generally don't like hot, dry or polluted conditions. Spruce are best grown from small, young stock as they dislike being transplanted when larger or more mature.

Tips
Spruce are used as specimen trees. The dwarf and slow-growing cultivars can also be used in shrub or mixed borders. These trees look most attractive when allowed to keep their lower branches.

Recommended
Spruce are generally upright, pyramidal trees, but cultivars may be low-growing, wide-spreading or even weeping in habit. *P. abies* (Norway spruce), *P. glauca* (white spruce), *P. pungens* (Colorado spruce) and their cultivars are popular and commonly available.

Oil-based pesticides such as dormant oil can take the blue out of your blue-needled spruce.

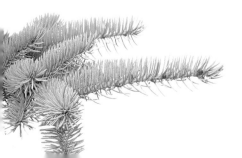

Features: foliage; cones; habit
Habit: conical or columnar, evergreen tree or shrub **Height:** 2–65' **Spread:** 2–30'
Hardiness: zones 2–8

Sumac

Rhus

Sumacs are unique foliar specimens that are ideally suited to contemporary designs where they can exhibit their colorful attributes and architectural form.

Growing

Sumacs develop the best fall color in **full sun,** but they tolerate partial shade. They prefer soil that is of **average fertility**, **moist** and **well drained**. Once established, sumacs tolerate drought very well.

Tips

Sumacs can be used to form a specimen group in a shrub or mixed border, on a sloping bank or in a woodland garden. Both male and female plants are needed for fruit to form.

Recommended

R. glabra (smooth sumac) is an upright, spreading shrub that grows in colonies as it suckers. The green foliage turns orange, red and purple in fall. Scarlet fruit follows the flowers. Various cultivars are available. (Zones 2–8)

R. trilobata (skunkbush sumac) is a slow-growing, upright shrub of medium size. It bears fragrant leaves, when crushed, and they turn a brilliant auburn red in fall. Cultivars are available in a spreading form.

R. typhina (*R. hirta*; staghorn sumac) is a suckering, colony-forming shrub

R. typhina (above & below)

with branches covered with velvety fuzz. Fuzzy, yellow, early-summer flowers are followed by hairy, red fruit. The leaves turn stunning shades of yellow, orange and red in fall.

Features: summer and fall foliage; flowers; fall fruit **Habit:** upright to low-growing, open, deciduous, spreading shrub **Flower color:** greenish yellow **Height:** 2–10' **Spread:** 7–13' **Hardiness:** zones 3–8

Viburnum
Viburnum

V. opulus 'Nanum' (above); V. lantana 'Mohican' (below)

Good fall color, attractive form, shade tolerance, scented flowers and attractive fruit put viburnums in a class by themselves.

Growing

Viburnums grow well in **full sun, partial shade** or **light shade**. The soil should be of **average fertility, moist** and **well drained**. Viburnums tolerate both alkaline and acidic soils.

These plants will look neatest if dead-headed, but this practice will prevent fruits from forming. Fruiting is better when more than one plant of a species is grown.

Tips

Viburnums can be used in borders and woodland gardens. They are a good choice for planting near decks and patios.

Recommended

Many viburnum species, hybrids and cultivars are available. *V. dentatum* (arrowwood) is a large shrub with coarse leaves and white flowers, followed by rounded, bluish black fruit. *V. lantana* (wayfaring tree) is a stout, globe-shaped shrub with leathery, gray-green foliage that turns purplish red in fall. Clusters of creamy white flowers emerge in spring, followed by reddish black berries. *V. lentago* (nannyberry) is a large, upright shrub that produces shiny, green foliage that turns a deep purple-red in fall. Flat-topped clusters of creamy white flowers emerge in spring, followed by bluish black berries. *V. opulus* (European cranberrybush, Guelder-rose) is a rounded, spreading, deciduous shrub with lacy-looking flower clusters. *V. trilobum* (highbush cranberry) is a dense, rounded shrub with clusters of white flowers followed by edible, red fruit. Cultivars are available for each species in varied forms, sizes and overall appeal.

Features: flowers (some fragrant); summer and fall foliage; fruit **Habit:** bushy or spreading, evergreen, semi-evergreen or deciduous shrub **Flower color:** white **Height:** 2–20' **Spread:** 2–10' **Hardiness:** zones 2–8

Willow

Salix

These fast-growing, deciduous shrubs or trees can have colorful or twisted stems or foliage, and they come in a huge range of growth habits and sizes.

Growing

Willows grow best in **full sun**. The soil should be of **average fertility, moist** and **well drained**.

Tips

Large tree willows should be reserved for large spaces; they look particularly attractive near water features. Smaller willows can be used as small specimen trees or in shrub and mixed borders. Small and trailing forms can be included in rock gardens and along retaining walls.

Recommended

There is an endless array of willow tree and shrub species and cultivars to choose from. They can range from creeping, groundcover shrubs with colorful foliage to large shrubs with dense habits and graceful forms. The trees are often quite large and require a grand space to show off their attributes. Check your local garden center to discover all of the willow possibilities.

S. *purpurea* 'Pendula' (above); S. *purpurea* 'Nana' (below)

Willows are a moisture-loving species that thrive near ponds, streams, rivers and poorly drained sites in their native habitat.

Features: summer and fall foliage; stems; habit **Habit:** bushy or arching shrub, or spreading or weeping tree **Height:** 1–55' **Spread:** 3–55' **Hardiness:** zones 2–8

Yew
Taxus

T. cuspidata (above & below)

From sweeping hedges to commanding specimens, yews can serve many purposes in the garden. They are some of the most reliable evergreens for deep shade.

Growing

Yews grow well in any light condition from **full sun to full shade**. The soil should be **fertile, moist** and **well drained**. They tolerate polluted conditions and soils of any acidity but cannot

Yews are better adapted to gardens in western Montana.

tolerate excessive soil moisture. They also dislike excessive heat, and on the hotter south or southwest side of a building they may suffer needle scorch.

Tips

Yews can be used in borders or as specimens, hedges, topiaries and groundcovers.

Male and female flowers are borne on separate plants. Both must be present for the attractive red seed cups to form.

Recommended

T. brevifolia (Pacific yew, western yew) is a large specimen with dark, yellowish green foliage. A few cultivars are available that offer columnar forms or a weeping habit.

T. canadensis (Canada yew, American yew) is a smaller shrub best suited to cool, shaded locations. It bears glossy, dark green foliage that takes on a reddish tint in winter.

T. cuspidata (Japanese yew) is an upright but irregularly V-shaped shrub with sharply pointed, needle-like leaves. A pyramidal cultivar is available.

T. x *media* (Anglojap yew), a cross between *T. baccata* (English yew) and *T. cuspidata* (Japanese yew), has the vigor of the English yew and the cold hardiness of the Japanese yew. It forms a rounded, upright tree or shrub, though the size and form can vary among the many cultivars. A few attractive selections include 'Andersonii,' 'Brownii,' 'Densiformis,' 'Hicksii' and 'Runyan.'

Features: foliage; habit; red seed cups
Habit: evergreen; conical or columnar tree, or bushy or spreading shrub **Height:** 2–45'
Spread: 1–35' **Hardiness:** zones 2–7

Champlain

Shrub, Explorer Rose

Champlain was bred by Felicitas Svejda in 1982 as part of a series Agriculture Canada developed to tolerate northern winters. It was a great success and remains one of the exceedingly popular Explorer series roses available today.

Growing

Champlain grows best in **full sun**. The soil should be preferably **average to fertile**, **humus rich, slightly acidic, moist** and **well drained**, but this durable rose adapts to most soils, from sandy to silty clay. Remove a few of the oldest canes every few years to keep the plants blooming vigorously.

Tips

This rose is well suited to mixed borders but is most effective when planted en masse. Champlain may require thorough pruning in spring to remove any deadwood. It will readily bush back out from the lower branches as summer wears on.

Champlain is reasonably resistant to blackspot and mildew. If subjected to extreme cold for two or three consecutive winters, it will experience dieback. It will begin to re-shoot within the same year but will have a shorter blooming period. Winter protection will help to reduce dieback.

Recommended

This moderately vigorous, repeat blooming shrub is compact, bushy and upright with a prolific blooming habit. Semi-double, lightly scented flowers of up of 30 petals each are borne in large, abundant clusters. The cup-shaped flowers are produced freely almost all season long. As the new, reddish foliage expands, each small leaflet forms a dense collection of shiny foliage that is unappealing to most insects, especially aphids.

Features: double flowers; habit; disease resistance **Flower color:** velvety red **Height:** 3–4' **Spread:** 3–4' **Hardiness:** zones 2b–9

Cuthbert Grant

Shrub, Parkland Rose

The blossoms, up to 4" wide, are strongly scented and will continue to emerge through a repeat blooming cycle.

This rose offers so much—prolific blooming, excellent disease resistance, luscious blossoms and a vigorous nature. What better rose package could you ask for?

Growing

This hardy Parkland rose requires **full sun** for a minimum of six hours daily. Most soils are adequate, but **organically rich, moist, well-drained** soils are best.

Tips

The rich-looking flowers are intensely fragrant and worthy of any garden setting. Cottage gardens and less formal gardens often suit this rose best, in mixed borders or left as a small specimen.

The process of deadheading is slightly different for this rose. Remove the entire cluster of flowers as they fade, rather than removing a single flower at a time. New, vigorous shoots will emerge once you remove any deadwood in spring.

Recommended

Cuthbert Grant is a bushy shrub and vigorous grower. Oval buds open into large, velvety, semi-double clusters of cupped flowers. The blooms are accompanied by glossy, disease-resistant foliage produced on upright, vigorous stems.

Features: flowers; habit; hardiness **Flower color:** crimson red **Height:** 3–4' **Spread:** 3–4' **Hardiness:** zones 3–9

Grootendorst Supreme

Shrub, Rugosa Rose

This rose bears carnation-like blossoms and provides a wonderful display of color in the garden all summer.

Growing

This hybrid rugosa prefers **full sun**. Most soils are adequate but **organically rich, moist, well-drained** soils are best.

Tips

This proven winner is well suited to a mixed border or used en masse as a hedge, not only for esthetic reasons, but also for the thorny canes which will deter people from walking through certain areas.

Recommended

R. **'Grootendorst Supreme'** is a vigorous, upright shrub with large, full clusters of small, dark red, double blooms that resemble carnations more than roses. It is considered to be one of the most continuous of bloomers. The coarsely textured, healthy foliage emerges from thorny canes.

Grootendorst Supreme is the dark red sport of the Grootendorst family of roses. They are known to be exceedingly disease resistant, hardy and floriferous.

Features: blooming habit; small, fringed flowers
Flower color: dark red **Height:** 4–5'
Spread: 4–5' **Hardiness:** zones 3–8

Hansa

Shrub, Rugosa Rose

Hansa, first introduced in 1905, is one of the most durable, long-lived and versatile roses.

Growing

Hansa grows best in **full sun**. The soil should preferably be **average to fertile, humus rich, slightly acidic, moist** and **well drained,** but this durable rose adapts to most soils, from sandy to silty clay. Remove a few of the oldest canes every few years to keep plants blooming vigorously.

Tips

Rugosa roses like Hansa make good additions to mixed borders and beds, and they can also be used as hedges or as specimens. Hansa is often used on steep banks to prevent soil erosion. Its prickly branches deter people from walking across flower beds and compacting the soil.

Recommended

Rosa 'Hansa' is a bushy shrub with arching canes and leathery, deeply veined, bright green leaves. Double flowers are produced all summer. The bright orange hips persist into winter. Other rugosa roses include **'Blanc Double de Coubert,'** which produces white, double flowers throughout summer.

Features: dense, arching habit; clove-scented, early-summer to fall flowers; orange-red hips **Flower color:** mauve purple or mauve red **Height:** 4–5' **Spread:** 5–6' **Hardiness:** zones 2–8

Harison's Yellow

Old Garden Rose, Hybrid Foetida

This rose first appeared in 1830, in an area that is now downtown Manhattan, NY, in the garden of attorney and amateur hybridist George F. Harison. Harison's Yellow was carried by a number of pioneers on their journeys west, and it remains as popular today as it was then.

Growing

Harison's Yellow tolerates drought, light shade and poor soils but prefers **full sun**. It may bloom more heavily in dry, cool locations.

Tips

Known to spread quickly by suckers, this rose is easily propagated by planting the suckers separately as new plants. It can also be divided in the same way as a perennial, with a shovel and a hatchet, and shared with friends.

Recommended

R. **'Harison's Yellow'** bears 2–2¹/₂" double, cupped blossoms along mahogany arching canes with many prickles. The canes form an open but bushy shrub. Each flower is made up of 20–24 petals surrounding showy, gold stamens. It puts on a brief but spectacular show early in the season and is often the first rose to bloom in spring. After the rose blooms, the ferny foliage remains attractive while black, bristly, oval hips form and last well into fall.

Also called: Harisonii, *R. foetida harisonii,* *R. lutea hoggii,* *R.* x *harisonii,* Pioneer Rose, *R.* x *harisonii* 'Harison's Yellow,' *R.* x *harisonii* 'Yellow Rose of Texas' **Features:** yellow blossoms; once blooming **Flower color:** bright yellow **Height:** 6–8' **Spread:** 5–7' **Hardiness:** zones 4–9

Henry Hudson

Shrub, Explorer Rose

The Explorer roses were developed by Agriculture Canada to be cold hardy and disease resistant. All the roses in this series have been named after early explorers.

Henry Hudson was introduced in 1976 and has proven to be easy to maintain. It is hardy and is resistant to mildew and blackspot.

Growing

Henry Hudson grows best in **full sun** but tolerates some afternoon shade. The soil should be **average to fertile, humus rich, slightly acidic, moist** and **well drained**. Deadhead to keep plants tidy.

Tips

With its thorny, impenetrable growth, Henry Hudson makes an attractive barrier plant, hedge or groundcover. It spreads by suckers and can be used on banks to prevent soil erosion. Henry Hudson also looks attractive in mixed beds or borders.

Recommended

Rosa 'Henry Hudson' is a spreading, rounded shrub with bright green foliage and semi-double flowers produced profusely all summer. Roses in the Explorer series come in a variety of flower colors and sizes, including climbers.

Features: rounded habit; clove-scented, early-summer to fall flowers **Flower color:** white **Height:** 24–36" **Spread:** 2–5' **Hardiness:** zones 2–8

Jens Munk

Shrub, Explorer Rose

The American Rose Society doesn't bestow the 'highly recommended' classification on just any rose. This tough and dependable Explorer rose is favored by both ARS rose enthusiasts and northern gardeners.

Growing

Jens Munk grows best in **full to partial sun**. It prefers a **fertile**, **moist** but **well-drained**, **slightly acidic** soil.

Tips

With its vast number of prickles, Jens Munk makes an impenetrable, medium-sized hedge. It blends beautifully into mixed beds and borders, or works well as a specimen.

Recommended

Rosa 'Jens Munk' grows vigorously into a rounded, dense shrub. It has a sprawling and unshapely form when young but evens out with maturity. Bright red hips follow the semi-double flowers. The wrinkly, shiny foliage turns a beautiful yellow-orange hue in fall.

This rose is extremely tough, highly disease resistant and drought tolerant. It requires very little to no maintenance.

Features: upright habit; spicy-scented, summer blossoms that repeat in fall **Flower color:** medium pink, purple **Height:** 5–7' **Spread:** 4–5' **Hardiness:** zones 3–8

John Cabot

Shrub, Explorer Rose

This rose was named after the first European since the Vikings to explore the North American mainland in search of the Northwest Passage. It is considered one of the best Explorer roses, exhibiting semi-double clusters of blooms that fade to pale pink over time.

Growing

John Cabot requires **partial to full sun**. The soil should be **average to fertile**, **slightly acidic**, **humus rich**, **moist** and **well drained**.

Tips

This rose variety works best when trained as a climber, but it can be pruned into a smaller specimen once it has finished flowering. Train the branches to climb on a decorative support such as a pergola, archway, trellis or obelisk.

Recommended

Rosa 'John Cabot' is a vigorous, tough rose that requires little maintenance and has good resistance to blackspot and powdery mildew. The prominent yellow stamens stand out among the cupped petals and light green foliage. The flower color can range from deep pink to reddish purple.

John Cabot was introduced in 1978 as the first climbing rose in the Explorer series.

Features: sweetly scented, mid-summer blossoms that repeat in fall **Flower color:** deep, vivid, magenta pink; reddish purple **Height:** 8–10' **Spread:** 5–6' **Hardiness:** zones 3–8

John Franklin

Shrub, Explorer Rose

*J*ohn Franklin has a slightly different flowering habit than other Explorer roses. It is an everblooming rose, meaning that rather than repeat blooming, it blooms continuously from summer to fall. The bright red flowers just keep coming, rain or shine, until the cool fall days finally slow it down.

Growing

John Franklin tolerates shade but prefers **partial to full sun**. The soil should be a **fertile, well-drained, moisture-holding loam** with at least 5% organic matter.

Tips

John Franklin's compact, bushy form makes this rose useful for hedging, borders and smaller gardens. It is ideal for those tight spaces that need a punch of color.

Recommended

Rosa '**John Franklin**' bears tight buds that open to semi-double flowers. The small, fringed flowers are borne in large, abundant clusters of 30 or more. The leaves are serrated and dark green with touches of burgundy around the edges.

This rose was named after a well-known British naval officer and northern explorer who is remembered for his expeditions and for the highly publicized 12-year search for him and his lost ships in the mid-1800s.

Features: compact, bushy form; lightly scented blossoms that bloom from spring to fall **Flower color:** medium red **Height:** 5' **Spread:** 4' **Hardiness:** zones 3–8

Martin Frobisher

Shrub, Explorer Rose

In 1968, Martin Frobisher became the first rose to be introduced in the Canadian Explorer series. It has the appearance of an old rose but has a few unique physical features—the older growth is covered in reddish brown bark, the upper portions of the branches are spineless and it does not form hips.

Growing

Martin Frobisher prefers at least five or six hours of **full sun** daily. The soil should be **well drained**, **slightly acidic**, **humus rich** and **moist**.

Tips

This upright shrub rose works well in mixed borders but is also effective left as a specimen.

Recommended

Rosa '**Martin Frobisher**' bears intensely fragrant, double flowers that open from well-shaped buds. It is a vigorous, dense, compact, well-proportioned, pillar-shaped shrub. Smooth, dark red stems display wrinkly, grayish green leaves.

Martin Frobisher was an Elizabethan seafaring explorer who, while he was searching for the Northwest Passage in 1576, discovered what is now known as Frobisher Bay on Baffin Island.

Features: tall, upright form; intensely scented, early summer blossoms that repeat in fall **Flower color:** pale pink **Height:** 5–6' **Spread:** 4–5' **Hardiness:** zones 2–8

Morden Blush

Shrub, Parkland Rose

Its pale pink, delicate blooms may lead you to believe that this rose is tender, but Morden Blush tolerates drought and extreme temperatures. It is heat and cold hardy, disease resistant and vigorous.

Growing

Morden Blush grows best in **full to partial sun.** It prefers a deep, **well-drained loam rich in organic matter** and **slightly acidic.**

Tips

The blooms are frequently used for corsages and bouquets; landscape uses include mass plantings, borders and mixed beds. Place Morden Blush in a well-ventilated area and water at the base of the plant in the morning to prevent the onset of disease.

Features: small, compact size; tea-scented, late-spring blossoms that continue throughout fall **Flower color:** pale pink **Height:** 24–36" **Spread:** 24–36" **Hardiness:** zones 2b–8

Recommended

Rosa 'Morden Blush' is a small shrub that bears attractive buds, which open flat into fully double sprays of rosette-shaped clusters. Each petal is in-folded, forming into a muddled, button-shaped center.

Introduced in 1988, Morden Blush is the longest-blooming, prairie-developed shrub rose to date. It was created in Canada by Collicutt & Marshall.

Morden Fireglow

Shrub, Parkland Rose

This rose is truly one of our favorites. One of the Parkland series, this hardy specimen bears flowers that are neither red nor orange—a color unlike that of any other hardy shrub rose.

This plant is considered self-cleaning because the petals fall cleanly from the plant once they've finished blooming.

Growing

Morden Fireglow prefers at least five or six hours of **full sun** per day. The soil should be **moist**, **well drained**, **slightly acidic** and **organically rich**.

Tips

Morden Fireglow will stand out among a variety of sun-loving plants, making it ideal for mixed beds and borders. Cut the stems while the flowers are still buds to extend the longevity of the cut flowers in bouquets.

Recommended

Rosa 'Morden Fireglow' is an upright shrub that bears double blossoms formed in loosely cupped sprays. The large, globular hips that form in fall remain on the plant well into the following spring.

Features: unique flower color; upright form; early-summer flowers that repeat in fall **Flower color:** deep scarlet red with orange **Height:** 2–4' **Spread:** 24–36" **Hardiness:** zones 2b–8

Morden Sunrise

Shrub, Parkland Rose

Morden Sunrise is the most adorable semi-double rose we've seen in recent years. Its 1999 introduction was highly anticipated, and the public received it very well. It remains as popular today as it was in the year of its introduction.

Growing
Morden Sunrise prefers **full sun**. The soil should be **well drained** but **moist**, **slightly acidic** and **rich with organic matter**.

Tips
This rose is ideal for borders and mixed beds, or grown as a specimen. Morden Sunrise is a colorful addition to just about any garden setting.

Recommended
Rosa '**Morden Sunrise**' is a compact shrub featuring erect stems, dense foliage and semi-double flowers. The first yellow variety in the Parkland series, it has a clean and fresh look, with blooms in tones of apricot and yellow, along with attractive, shiny, dark green leaves.

Cooler temperatures cause the flower color to intensify, while hotter weather results in paler, softer tones.

Features: compact size; lightly scented, apricot flowers that emerge in early summer and again in fall **Flower color:** apricot yellow
Height: 24–30" **Spread:** 24–30"
Hardiness: zones 3–8

Red-Leafed Rose
Species Rose

This rose thrives where most plants could not survive. The starry, pink blossoms make a striking contrast to the violet-tinted foliage. The foliage sometimes appears to change color, depending on the degree of sun exposure.

Growing
Red-leafed Rose tolerates shade but prefers **full sun**. Most soils are fine, but **well drained**, **moist**, **slightly acidic** soil is best. Keep this species under control with regular pruning, which will encourage new and colorful shoots.

Tips
Red-leafed Rose makes an ideal hedge because of its vigorous nature and arching, thorny, purple stems. Its burgundy hips and maroon stems lend color to a stark winter landscape. It also makes a splendid specimen.

Recommended
Red-leafed Rose (R. glauca) is extremely popular among rosarians and novice gardeners alike because it is so hardy and disease resistant. Its flowers are followed by clusters of small, rounded, dark red hips that remain on the shrub well into the following spring.

Red-leafed Rose is sought after by floral designers for its colorful, dainty foliage, which is perfect for floral arrangements.

Features: tall, upright form; single flowers emerge in late spring and continue to bloom until summer **Flower color:** mauve-pink with white centers **Height:** 6–10' **Spread:** 5–6' **Hardiness:** zones 2–8

Thérèse Bugnet

Shrub, Rugosa rose

One of the cold-hardiest roses in the world, Thérèse Bugnet endures temperatures of –35° F and still produces luxurious sprays of pink flowers almost all summer long.

Growing

Thérèse Bugnet doesn't mind **partial shade to full sun**, **alkaline**, **rocky**, **sandy** or **clay** soils or neglect. This exceptional rugosa variety tolerates cold and heat and late frosts.

Tips

This hardy rose is well suited to both mixed borders and beds, or left as a specimen.

Like other rugosas, Thérèse Bugnet resents being sprayed with fungicides. If powdery mildew occurs, prune out and destroy infected growth. Deadheading regularly and pruning after the first flowering cycle in early summer will prolong the blooming cycle. Otherwise, the only pruning required is to cut the magnificent flowers for arrangements.

Recommended

R. **'Thérèse Bugnet'** is a little hesitant to bloom when young, but it's well worth the wait. Once established, or when it is at least two or three years of age, it will produce gray-green, rather smooth leaves on almost thornless canes. The stems are tipped with a profusion of ruffled, double, lilac pink blossoms that pale with age. After the flowers have all but finished, attractive fall color prevails with cherry red canes, orange hips and bronzed foliage.

Features: blossoms; blooming habit; hardiness
Flower color: medium lilac pink **Height:** 5–6'
Spread: 5–6' **Hardiness zones:** 2–9

William Baffin

Explorer Shrub Rose

Tough and versatile, hardy and vigorous, this rose meets all expectations. William Baffin is highly disease resistant and requires little to no maintenance. It is thought to be the best shrub or climbing rose for colder regions.

Growing

William Baffin prefers **full sun** but tolerates afternoon shade. **Average to fertile, slightly acidic** soil that's **rich with organic matter** works best. The soil should also be **moist** and **well drained**.

Tips

William Baffin is tall enough to be trained as a climber or pillar rose. It is hardy enough to remain on a trellis, arbor or pergola in the coldest of winters, but protection must be provided against wind and bright sunlight.

Recommended

Rosa **'William Baffin'** bears semi-double flowers in clusters of 30 or more. Glossy, medium-green foliage is vigorously produced in dense mounds on stiff, wiry stems.

This rose was named after the famous explorer who discovered Lancaster Sound while he searched for the Northwest Passage in 1616.

Features: vigorous, hardy climber; lightly scented, summer flowers that repeat in fall
Flower color: deep pink **Height:** 8–10'
Spread: 5–6' **Hardiness:** zones 2–8

Bittersweet

Celastrus

Bittersweet is a rough-and-tumble, low-maintenance, woody climber that lends a wild look to the garden. Highly decorative clusters of fruit burst forth in fall.

Growing

Bittersweet grows well in **full sun** but tolerates partial shade. It prefers **poor soil** but adapts to almost any **well-drained** soil. Bittersweet does best in areas with higher humidity levels.

Male and female flowers usually bloom on separate plants. Bittersweet is often sold with a male and a female plant in one pot. Both sexes, planted in close proximity, are needed for fruit production. Water them well.

Tips

Bittersweet belongs at the edge of a woodland garden and in a naturalized area. It quickly covers fences, arbors, trellises, posts and walls. As a groundcover it can mask rubble and tree stumps, and effectively controls erosion on hard-to-maintain slopes. All parts of bittersweet are said to be poisonous.

This vine can damage or kill young trees or shrubs if allowed to twine around the stems.

Recommended

C. scandens (American bittersweet, staff vine) is a vigorous, twining vine with dark green, glossy foliage that turns bright yellow in fall. Small, yellow-green to whitish flowers bloom in late spring followed by showy fruit. '**Indian Brave**' and '**Indian Maid,**' the male and female cultivar pair, are hardier than the species.

Generally, one male plant will pollinate six to nine female plants. The subsequent berry production is very attractive to birds.

Also called: American bittersweet
Features: fast growth; twining stems; fruit; fall color **Height:** 6½–10' **Spread:** 3–6'
Hardiness: zones 3–8

Clematis
Clematis

C. x *jackmanii* (above)

There are so many species, hybrids and cultivars of clematis that it is possible to have one in bloom all season.

Growing

Clematis plants prefer **full sun** but tolerate partial shade. The soil should be **fertile, humus rich, moist** and **well drained**. These vines enjoy warm, sunny weather, but the roots prefer to be cool. A thick layer of mulch or a planting of low, shade-providing perennials will protect the tender roots. Clematis are quite cold hardy but will fare best when protected from winter wind. The rootball of vining

clematis should be planted about 2" beneath the soil surface.

Tips

Clematis vines can climb up structures such as trellises, railings, fences and arbors. They can also be allowed to grow over shrubs and up trees and can be used as groundcover.

Recommended

There are many species, hybrids and cultivars of clematis but *C.* x *jackmanii* (Jackman clematis) is one of the most popular, and a hardy, vining clematis that blooms in mid- to late summer. The twining vines of this hybrid grow about 10' tall. Large, purple flowers appear on side shoots from the previous season and on new growth for most of summer.

Features: twining habit; early- to late-summer flowers; decorative seedheads **Flower color:** blue, purple, pink, yellow, red, white **Height:** 10–17' or more **Spread:** 5' or more **Hardiness:** zones 3–8

Dutchman's Pipe

Aristolochia

*O*f exotic is what you're looking for, then look no further. This unusual, vigorous climber bears pipe-shaped flowers that are sure to the topic of conversation at your next garden party.

Growing

Dutchman's pipe grows well in **full sun** or **partial shade** and in **fertile, well-drained soil**. Provide a sturdy support for the vines to twine up. It can be cut back as needed during the growing season and should be thinned to a strong frame of main branches in late fall or spring.

Tips

These vines are grown on trellises, arbors and buildings as quick-growing screens.

This vine will die back over the winter months and mulching for added winter protection is a must. Some gardeners treat this vine as an annual and propagate it with cuttings or seeds from one year to the next to ensure its survival.

A. macrophylla (above & below)

Recommended

A. macrophylla (*A. durior*) is a deciduous, twining vine. It provides a dense curtain of large, heart-shaped leaves that often hides the unusual, pipe-shaped flowers. Some people find the scent of the flowers unpleasant.

Butterflies adore the flowers of Dutchman's pipe.

Features: unusual, exotic flowers; heart-shaped leaves; twining habit; attract pollinating insect **Flower color:** mid-green, mottled with yellow, purple and brown **Height:** 20–30' **Spread:** 20–30' **Hardiness:** zones 5–8

English Ivy
Hedera

H. helix (above & below)

English ivy is also a popular houseplant.

One of the loveliest things about English ivy is the variation in green and blue tones it adds to the garden.

Growing

English ivy prefers **light or partial shade** but will adapt to any light condition, from full shade to full sun. The foliage can become damaged or dried out in winter if the plant is growing in a sunny, exposed site. The soil should be of **average to rich fertility, moist** and **well drained**. The richer the soil, the better this vine will grow.

Tips

English ivy is grown as a trailing groundcover or as a climbing vine. It clings tenaciously to house walls, tree trunks and rough-textured surfaces. Ivy rootlets can damage walls and fences, but cold Montana winters prevent the rampant growth that makes this plant troublesome and invasive in warmer climates.

Recommended

H. helix is a vigorous plant with dark, glossy, triangular, evergreen leaves that may be tinged with bronze or purple in winter. Many cultivars have been developed. Some are popular for their increased cold hardiness. Others have interesting, often variegated, foliage but are not exceptionally hardy. Check with your local garden center to see what is available.

Features: foliage; climbing or trailing habit
Height: indefinite **Spread:** indefinite
Hardiness: zones 5–8

Hardy Kiwi
Actinidia

Hardy kiwi is handsome in its simplicity. Its lush green leaves, vigor and adaptability make it very useful, especially in difficult sites.

Growing

Hardy kiwi vines grow best in **full sun**. The soil should be **fertile** and **well drained**. These plants require shelter from strong winds.

Tips

These vines need a sturdy structure to twine around. Pergolas, arbors and sufficiently large and sturdy fences provide good support. Given a trellis against a wall, a tree or some other upright structure, hardy kiwis will twine upward all summer. They can also be grown in containers.

Hardy kiwi vines can grow uncontrollably. Don't be afraid to prune them back if they get out of hand.

Recommended

Two hardy kiwi vines are grown in Montana gardens. *A. arguta* (hardy kiwi, bower actinidia) has dark green, heart-shaped leaves, white flowers and smooth-skinned, greenish yellow edible fruit. *A. kolomikta* (variegated kiwi vine, kolomikta actinidia) has green leaves strongly variegated with pink and white, smooth-skinned, greenish yellow edible fruit and white flowers.

A. kolomikta (above), *A. arguta* 'Ananasaya' (below)

Features: early-summer flowers; edible fruit; twining habit
Height: 15–30' to indefinite
Flower colour: white
Spread: 15–30' to indefinite
Hardiness: zones 3–8

Both a male and a female vine must be present for fruit to be produced. The plants are often sold in pairs.

Honeysuckle

Lonicera

L. sempervirens (above); L. x brownii

Honeysuckle flowers are often scented and attract hummingbirds as well as bees and other pollinating insects.

Honeysuckles can be rampant twining vines, but with careful consideration and placement they won't overrun your garden. The fragrance of the flowers makes any effort worthwhile.

Growing

Honeysuckles grow well in **full sun** or **partial shade**. The soil should be **average to fertile, humus rich, moist** and **well drained**.

Tips

Honeysuckle can be trained to grow up a trellis, fence, arbor or other structure. In a large container near a porch it will ramble over the edges of the pot and up the railings with reckless abandon.

Recommended

There are dozens of honeysuckle species, hybrids and cultivars. Check with your local garden center to see what is available. The following are two popular species.

L.* x *brownii (scarlet trumpet honeysuckle) produces blue-green, rounded leaves and clusters of fiery, tubular flowers on the tips of twining stems. Many cultivars are available.

L. sempervirens (trumpet honeysuckle, coral honeysuckle) bears orange or red flowers in late spring and early summer. Many cultivars and hybrids are available. (Zones 4–8)

Features: late-spring and early-summer flowers; twining habit; fruit **Flower color:** orange, red **Height:** 6–15' **Spread:** 6–15' **Hardiness:** zones 3–8

Hops

Humulus

H. lupulus (above & below)

If you sit next to hops for an afternoon, you might actually be able to watch them grow.

Growing

Hops grow best in **full sun**. The soil should be **average to fertile, humus rich, moist** and **well drained**, though established plants will adapt to most conditions as long as they are well watered for the first few years.

Tips

Hops will quickly twine around any sturdy support to create a screen, or shade a patio or deck. Provide a pergola, arbor, porch rail or even a telephone pole for hops to grow up. Most trellises are too delicate for this vigorous grower.

Recommended

H. lupulus is a fast-growing, twining vine with rough-textured, bright green leaves and stems. The fragrant cone-like flowers—used to flavor beer—are produced only on the female plants. A cultivar with golden yellow foliage is available.

Wear protective gloves and long sleeves when handling hops to protect sensitive skin from rashes.

Features: twining habit; dense growth; cone-like, late-summer flowers **Flower color:** pale green turning to beige **Height:** 10–20' **Spread:** 10–20' **Hardiness:** zones 3–8

Morning Glory

Ipomoea

I. alba (above & below)

Morning glory will embellish a chain-link fence, a wire topiary structure or any object thin enough to twine its tendrils around. Once established, stand back—this vine grows fast.

Growing

Grow morning glory in **full sun** in **light, well-drained** soil of **poor fertility**. It tolerates any type of soil. Soak seeds for 24 hours before sowing. Start seeds in individual peat pots if sowing indoors. Plant in late spring.

Tips

Morning glory can be grown anywhere: fences, walls, trees, trellises or arbors. As a groundcover, it will cover any obstacles it encounters.

This vine must twine around objects, such as wire or twine, in order to climb. Wide fence posts, walls or other broad objects are too large.

Recommended

I. alba (moonflower) has sweet-scented, white flowers that open at night.

I. purpurea (common morning glory) bears trumpet-shaped flowers in purple, blue, pink or white.

I. tricolor (morning glory) produces purple or blue flowers with white centers. Many cultivars are available.

Features: fast growth **Habit:** herbaceous, twining vine or groundcover **Flower color:** white, blue, pink, purple, variegated **Height:** 10–12' **Spread:** 12–24" **Hardiness:** grown as annual

Scarlet Runner Bean

Phaseolus

Scarlet runner bean is both functional and beautiful. It'll scramble up a support in no time at all, blooming throughout the summer months and producing buckets of beans good enough to eat.

Growing

Scarlet runner bean prefers to grow in **full sun** in **well-drained, fertile, moist** soil. Provide it with adequate water.

Tips

Scarlet runner bean is a twining climber and will need something to climb onto, such as a trellis, arbor or post. Attach some form of lattice or netting if you want scarlet runner bean to grow up a fence or building.

Recommended

P. coccineus is a fast-growing, twining vine that grows to a height of 6½–9'. It bears clusters of scarlet red flowers in summer. Dark green, edible pods follow flowering. Cultivars are available with red and white bicolored and solid white flowers.

P. coccineus (above & below)

These plants are at home in the flower garden as well as in the vegetable garden. The dark green pods are edible—they're tender when young but get a little tough with age. Pick the pods just after the flowers fade for the best taste in a stir-fry.

Features: flowers; twining habit; fruit **Flower color:** red, white, bicolored **Height:** 6–8' **Spread:** 8–10' **Hardiness:** grown as an annual

Silver Fleece Vine
Polygonum

P. aubertii (above & below)

Silver fleece vine blooms late in the growing season, in the sweltering days of late August and early September, when most plants have petered out.

This tender vine is extremely vigorous. The lush foliage and panicles of foamy white flowers will leave you wanting more.

Growing

Silver fleece vine prefers **full to partial sun**. It isn't fussy about soil conditions and tolerates a location with poor soil. More nutrient-rich, moist and well-drained soil will produce more vigorous vines.

Tips

Silver fleece vine is ideal for adorning arbors, large obelisks and pergolas. The tiny, creamy white flowers are slightly fragrant and should be grown near a bench or patio breakfast nook, where their aroma can be enjoyed.

This vine should be pruned to the ground in fall or early spring before the new growth begins to emerge.

Recommended

P. aubertii is a tender vine with bright green, heart-shaped leaves that densely clothe the twining stems. Large panicles of creamy white flowers emerge in late summer and emit a delightful scent.

Also called: Russian vine, China fleece vine, silver lace vine **Features:** vigorous habit; scented flowers; lush foliage **Flower color:** creamy white **Height:** 10–15' **Spread:** depends on support **Hardiness:** zones 5–8; grown as an annual

Sweet Pea
Lathyrus

Sweet peas are among the most enchanting annuals. Their fragrance is intoxicating, and the flowers in double tones and shimmering shades resemble no other annual in the garden.

Growing

Sweet peas prefer **full sun** but tolerate light shade. The soil should be **fertile,** high in **organic matter, moist** and **well drained**. The plants tolerate light frost.

Soak seeds in water for 24 hours or nick them with a nail file before planting them. Planting a second crop of sweet peas about a month after the first one will ensure a longer blooming period. Deadhead all blooms.

Tips

Sweet peas will grow up poles, trellises, fences or over rocks. They cling by wrapping tendrils around whatever they are growing up, so they do best when they have a rough surface, chain-link fence, small twigs or a net to cling to.

Recommended

There are many cultivars of **L. odoratus** available, though many are small and bushy rather than climbing. **'Bouquet'** is a tall, climbing variety with flowers in a wide range of colors.

L. odoratus cultivars (above & below)

The newer sweet pea cultivars often have less fragrant flowers than the old-fashioned cultivars. Look for heritage varieties to enjoy the most fragrant flowers.

Features: clinging habit; summer flowers **Flower color:** pink, red, purple, lavender, blue, salmon, pale yellow, peach, white, bicolored **Height:** 12"–6' **Spread:** 6–12" **Hardiness:** hardy annual

Virginia Creeper
Parthenocissus

P. quinquefolia (above & below)

Virginia creeper and Boston ivy are handsome vines that establish quickly and provide an air of age and permanence, even on new structures.

Growing

These vines grow well in any light, from **full sun to full shade**. The soil should be **fertile** and **well drained**. The plants adapt to clay or sandy soils.

Tips

Virginia creepers can cover an entire building, given enough time. They do not require support because they have clinging rootlets that can adhere to just about any surface, even smooth wood, vinyl or metal. Give the plants a lot of space and let them cover a wall, fence or arbor.

Recommended

P. quinquefolia (Virginia creeper, woodbine) has dark green foliage. Each leaf, divided into five leaflets, turns flame red in fall. *P. quinquefolia* var. *engelmannii* (Engelman ivy) is another self-clinging variety, but unlike the species, it uses adhesive pads rather than tendrils to attach itself to supports or surfaces. This variety is as colorful and vigorous as the species, but far more resistant to powdery mildew. Don't grow it against wooden structures or surfaces that will require maintenance. (Zones 3–9)

P. tricuspidata (Boston ivy) produces glossy, dark green foliage reminiscent of grape leaves. The foliage turns shades of orange and red in fall. This self-climber can grow quite tall in a short time. (Zones 4–9)

Features: summer and fall foliage; clinging habit **Height:** 30–70' **Spread:** 30–70' **Hardiness:** zones 3–8

Crocus

Crocus

C. x *vernus* cultivars (above & below)

Crocuses are harbingers of spring. They often appear, as if by magic, in full bloom from beneath the melting snow.

Growing

Crocuses grow well in **full sun** or **light, dappled shade**. The soil should be of **poor to average fertility, gritty** and **well drained**. The corms are planted about 4" deep in fall. Foliage should be left in place after the plants flower but can be cut back once it begins to wither and turn brown in summer.

Tips

Crocuses are almost always planted in groups. Drifts of crocuses can be planted in lawns to provide interest and color while the grass still lies dormant. After the foliage withers in mid-June, crocuses may be mowed over. In beds and borders they can be left to naturalize. Groups of plants will fill in and spread out to provide a bright welcome in spring. Plant perennials among the crocuses to fill in the gaps once the crocuses die back.

Recommended

Many crocus species, hybrids and cultivars are available. The spring-flowering crocus most people are familiar with is **C.** x **vernus**, commonly called Dutch crocus. Many cultivars are available with flowers in shades of purple, yellow and white, sometimes bicolored or with darker veins.

Features: early-spring flowers **Flower color:** purple, yellow, white, bicolored **Height:** 2–6" **Spread:** 2–4" **Hardiness:** zones 3–8

Daffodil

Narcissus

Many gardeners automatically think of large, yellow, trumpet-shaped flowers when they think of daffodils, but there is a lot of variety in color, form and size among the daffodils.

Growing

Daffodils grow best in **full sun** or **light, dappled shade**. The soil should be **average to fertile, moist** and **well drained**. Bulbs should be planted in fall, 2–8" deep, depending on the size of the bulb. The bigger the bulb, the deeper it should be planted. A rule of thumb is to measure the bulb from top to bottom and multiply that number by three to know how deeply to plant.

Tips

Daffodils are often planted where they can be left to naturalize, in the light shade beneath a tree or in a woodland garden. In mixed beds and borders, the faded leaves are hidden by the summer foliage of other plants.

Recommended

Many species, hybrids and cultivars of daffodils are available. Flowers come in shades of white, yellow, peach, orange and pink, and may be bicolored. Flowers may be 1½–6" across, solitary, or borne in clusters. There are 12 flower-form categories.

Features: spring flowers **Flower color:** white, yellow, peach, orange, pink, bicolored **Height:** 4–24" **Spread:** 4–12" **Hardiness:** zones 3–8

Frittilary

Frittillaria

Frittilary plants will offer a formal element to an otherwise casual setting, bearing unusual, royal-looking blossoms in early-summer.

Growing

Frittilary prefers **full sun** or **light shade** in an area sheltered from the wind. The soil should be **coarse, organically rich, moist** and **very well-drained**. It is important that the soil not be allowed to dry out during its dormant period in the midst of the growing season.

To protect frittilary bulbs from late-spring frosts, they should be planted 9" deep or more, and at least 4" apart from one another. Propagate by division, offsets and seed.

Tips

There are many frittilary species to choose from, but crown imperial frittilary can grow quite tall and has the most architectural appeal. Frittilaries are most striking when planted in large groupings at the back of mixed borders, where the scent may be a little less evident. They are best grown among shrubbery, where they won't be disturbed and will benefit from fallen leaf matter, both as a mulch and as organic matter.

Recommended

F. imperialis (crown imperial frittilary) is a true bulb that produces a lush cluster of blade-like leaves at the base of a tall, slender stalk. The stalk is bare up to the top, where a large

F. imperialis 'Lutea' (above); *F. imperialis* (below)

cluster of pendent, bell-shaped blossoms surround the tip, topped with a further cluster of green foliage. Many cultivars are available in fiery shades of orange, yellow and red.

Features: striking, pendent flowers in early to mid-summer; form Flower color: orange, yellow, red Height: 3–4' Spread: 6–12" Hardiness: zones 4–8

Gladiolus

Gladiolus

'Homecoming' (below)

Perhaps best known as a cut flower, gladiolus adds an air of extravagance to the garden.

Growing

Gladiolus grows best in **full sun** but tolerates partial shade. The soil should be **fertile, humus rich, moist** and **well drained**. Flower spikes may need staking and shelter from wind to prevent them from blowing over.

Plant corms in spring, 4–6" deep, once the soil has warmed. Corms can also be started early indoors. Plant a few corms each week for about a month to prolong the blooming period.

Tips

Planted in groups in beds and borders, gladiolus makes a bold statement. Dig up the corms in fall and store them in damp peat moss in a cool, frost-free location over the winter.

Recommended

G. x *hortulanus* is a huge group of hybrids. Gladiolus flowers come in almost every imaginable shade, except blue. Plants are commonly grouped in three classifications: **Grandiflorus** is the best known, each corm producing a single spike of large, often ruffled flowers; **Nanus**, the hardiest group, survives in zone 3 with protection and produces several spikes of up to seven flowers; and **Primulinus** produces a single spike of up to 23 flowers that grow more spaced out than those of the grandiflorus.

Features: brightly colored, mid- to late-summer flowers **Flower color:** all shades, except blue **Height:** 18"–6' **Spread:** 6–12" **Hardiness:** zone 8; grown as an annual

Grape Hyacinth

Muscari

Tulips should never be alone to signal the emergence of spring. Grape hyacinth bulbs are the perfect accompaniment to tulips and contrast beautifully with just about any color combination.

Growing

Grape hyacinth prefers **full sun to partial shade**. The soil should be **well drained** and **organically rich**.

Tips

Grape hyacinth is great for naturalizing. Plant individual bulbs random distances from one another in your lawn, but don't plan on cutting the grass until the grape hyacinth leaves have died down for another year. Grape hyacinth is also quite beautiful planted alongside perennials that will begin to envelop the tired-looking grape hyacinth foliage as they reach their full size for the season.

Recommended

M. armeniacum (Armenian grape hyacinth) is the most well-known species. It produces grass-like foliage and clusters of purple-blue, grape-like flowers atop slender, green stems. The flowers emit a strong, musky scent. **M. botryoides** (common grape hyacinth) is very similar in appearance in a slightly more compact form. It is less invasive than other species and will naturalize in a more respectable manner.

M. latifolium (bicolor muscari, giant grape hyacinth, one-leaf hyacinth) is a taller species that blooms a little later than the other species. It bears broader leaves and bicolored blooms. From each

M. armeniacum (above & below)

flower spike emerges two different kinds of flowers: smaller, sterile flowers in light blue towards the tip, and darker, fertile flowers further down.

M. neglectum (*M. racemosum;* musk hyacinth) bears clusters of deep, dark purple, vase-shaped flowers, with a distinctive white-edged rim on each individual flower.

Features: grape-like clusters of fragrant flowers; habit **Flower color:** blue, purple **Height:** 6–10" **Spread:** 6–8" **Hardiness:** zones 2–8

Tulip

Tulipa

Tulips, with their beautiful, often garishly colored flowers, are a welcome sight as we enjoy the warm days of spring.

Growing

Tulips grow best in **full sun**. The flowers tend to bend toward the light in light or partial shade. The soil should be **fertile** and **well drained**. Plant bulbs in fall, 4–6" deep, depending on size of bulb. Bulbs that have been cold treated can be planted in spring. Although tulips can repeat bloom, many hybrids perform best if planted new each year. Species and older cultivars are the best choice for naturalizing.

Tips

Tulips provide the best display when mass planted, or planted in groups in flowerbeds or borders. They can also be grown in containers and can be forced to bloom early in pots indoors. Some of the species and older cultivars can be naturalized in meadow and wildflower gardens.

Recommended

There are about 100 species of tulips and thousands of hybrids and cultivars. They are generally divided into 15 groups based on bloom time and flower appearance. They come in dozens of shades, with many bicolored or multi-colored varieties. Blue is the only shade not available. Check with your local garden center in early fall for the best selection.

Features: spring flowers **Flower color:** all colors, except blue **Height:** 6–30" **Spread:** 2–8" **Hardiness:** zones 3–8

Basil
Ocimum

The sweet, fragrant leaves of fresh basil add a delicious licorice-like flavor to salads and tomato-based dishes.

Growing

Basil grows best in a **warm, sheltered** location in **full sun**. The soil should be **fertile, moist** and **well drained**. Pinch tips regularly to encourage bushy growth. Plant out or direct sow seed after frost danger has passed in spring.

Tips

Although basil will grow best in a warm spot outdoors in the garden, it can be grown successfully in a pot by a bright window indoors to provide you with fresh leaves all year.

Recommended

O. basilicum is one of the most popular of the culinary herbs. There are dozens of varieties, including ones with large or tiny, green or purple and smooth or ruffled leaves.

O. basilicum 'Genovese' & 'Cinnamon' (above); 'Genovese' (below)

Basil is a good companion plant for tomatoes—both like warm, moist growing conditions—and when you pick tomatoes for a salad you'll also remember to include a few leaves of basil.

Features: fragrant, decorative leaves
Height: 12–24" **Spread:** 18"
Hardiness: tender annual

Borage
Borago

B. officinalis (above & below)

The young leaves of borage are yummy in cool, raw salads and in cold summer drinks, or they can be cooked with vegetables. The flowers can be candied for decorating desserts.

Borage is a vigorous, tenacious, annual herb. It is valued by some but disliked by others because of its natural inclination to reseed itself everywhere. The flowers and foliage are not only pretty, but are also useful in salads and desserts.

Growing

Borage prefers **full sun**. **Moist, sandy, well-drained** soil is best. Borage is drought tolerant once established. Remove any unwanted seedlings as they emerge in early spring to prevent an onslaught of plants.

Tips

Plant borage in your vegetable or herb garden to attract bees for pollination. As an ornamental, borage contrasts beautifully with dark foliage specimens.

Recommended

B. officinalis is an upright plant with high clusters of pendent, violet blue flowers in spring. The stems and foliage are covered in silvery hairs that complement the bluish flowers.

Features: flowers; habit; fuzzy foliage and stems **Flower color:** violet blue **Height:** 24–36" **Spread:** 24" **Hardiness:** zones 5–10

Chives

Allium

A. schoenoprasum (above & below)

The delicate onion flavor of chives is best enjoyed fresh. Mix chives into dips or sprinkle them on salads and baked potatoes.

Growing

Chives grow best in **full sun**. The soil should be **fertile, moist** and **well drained**, but chives adapt to most soil conditions. These plants are easy to start from seed, but they do like the soil temperature to stay above 65° F before they will germinate, so seeds started directly in the garden are unlikely to sprout before early summer.

Tips

Chives are decorative enough to be included in a mixed or herbaceous border and can be left to naturalize. In a herb garden, chives should be given plenty of space to allow self-seeding and spreading.

Recommended

A. schoenoprasum forms a clump of bright green, cylindrical leaves. Clusters of pinky purple flowers are produced in early and mid-summer. Varieties with white or pink flowers are available.

Chives are said to increase appetite and encourage good digestion.

Features: foliage; form; flowers **Flower color:** white, pink, purple **Height:** 8–24" **Spread:** 12" or more **Hardiness:** zones 3–8

Common Sage

Salvia

'Icterina' (above); 'Purpurea' (below)

Sage has been used since at least ancient Greek times as a medicinal and culinary herb and continues to be widely used for both of these purposes today.

Sage is perhaps best known as a flavoring for stuffings, but it has a great range of uses and can be added to soups, stews, sausages and dumplings.

Growing

Sage prefers **full sun** but tolerates light shade. The soil should be of **average fertility** and **well drained**. Sage benefits from a light mulch of compost each year. It is drought tolerant once established.

Tips

Sage is an attractive plant for the border, adding volume to the middle of the border or as an attractive edging or feature plant near the front. Sage can also be grown in mixed planters.

Recommended

S. officinalis is a woody, mounding plant with soft, gray-green leaves. Spikes of light purple flowers appear in early and mid-summer. Many cultivars with attractive foliage are available, including the silver-leaved **'Berggarten,'** the purple-leaved **'Purpurea,'** the yellow-margined **'Icterina,'** and the purple-green and cream variegated **'Tricolor,'** whose new growth has a pink flush.

Features: fragrant, decorative foliage; summer flowers **Flower color:** blue, purple **Height:** 12–24" **Spread:** 18–36" **Hardiness:** zones 4–8

Coriander·Cilantro
Coriandrum

Coriander is a multi-purpose herb. The leaves are called cilantro and are used in salads, salsas and soups; the seeds are called coriander and are used in pies, chutneys and marmalades.

Growing
Coriander prefers **full sun** but tolerates partial shade. The soil should be **fertile, light** and **well drained**. This plant dislikes humid conditions and does best during a dry summer.

Tips
Coriander has pungent leaves and is best planted where people will not have to brush past it. It is, however, a delight to behold when in flower. Add a plant or two here and there throughout your borders and vegetable garden, both for the visual appeal and to attract beneficial insects.

Recommended
C. sativum forms a clump of lacy, basal foliage above which large, loose clusters of tiny, white flowers are produced. The seeds ripen in late summer and fall.

The delicate, cloud-like clusters of flowers attract pollinating insects, such as butterflies and bees, as well as abundant predatory insects that will help keep pest insects at a minimum in your garden.

C. sativum (above & below)

Features: form; foliage; flowers; seeds
Flower color: white **Height:** 16–24"
Spread: 8–16" **Hardiness:** tender annual

Dill
Anethum

Dill turns up frequently in historical records as being both a culinary and a medicinal herb. It was used by the Egyptians and Romans, and it is mentioned in the Bible.

Dill leaves and seeds are probably best known for their use as pickling herbs, though they have a wide variety of other culinary uses.

Growing
Dill grows best in **full sun** in a **sheltered** location out of strong winds. The soil should be of **poor to average fertility, moist** and **well drained.** Sow seeds every few weeks in spring and early summer to ensure a regular supply of leaves.

Dill should not be grown near fennel because they will cross-pollinate and the seeds will lose their distinct flavors.

Tips
With its feathery leaves, dill is an attractive addition to a mixed bed or border. It can be included in a vegetable garden but does well in any sunny location. It also attracts predatory insects to the garden.

Recommended
A. graveolens forms a clump of feathery foliage. Clusters of yellow flowers are borne at the tops of sturdy stems.

Features: feathery, edible foliage; summer flowers; edible seeds **Flower color:** yellow **Height:** 2–5' **Spread:** 12" or more **Hardiness:** annual

Lavender

Lavandula

L. angustifolia (above & below)

All parts of the lavender plant are aromatic. The aroma is intensified when the foliage or flowers are touched, whether fresh or dried. The scent will evoke memories of warm summer days, even in the depths of winter.

Growing

Lavender grows best in **full sun**. The soil should be **average to fertile**, **alkaline** and **well drained**. In colder areas, lavender should be covered with mulch and a good layer of snow. The key to winter survival is good drainage—winterkill often results from wet 'feet,' not from the cold.

Tips

Lavenders are wonderful edging plants. Other drought-tolerant specimens, such as pinks, thyme, lamb's ears and sedum, make good companions for these deer-resistant plants.

Recommended

L. angustifolia is an aromatic, bushy, tender perennial. From mid-summer to fall it bears spikes of small flowers in varied shades of violet blue that stand above fragrant, silvery green foliage.

Also called: English lavender **Features:** fragrant flower spikes; silvery foliage **Flower color:** purple, pink, blue **Height:** 8–24" **Spread:** 12–24" **Hardiness:** zones 5–9

Lemon Verbena
Aloysia

A. triphylla (above & below)

Aloysia was named after the Princess of Parma, Maria Louisa, who died in 1819. Lemon verbena was commonly known as 'the lemon plant' in the Victorian era.

Lemon verbena has a wide variety of uses. Its fresh leaves can be used to flavor oils and vinegars, drinks, desserts and stuffings, or made into fragrant sachets for year-round enjoyment.

Growing
Lemon verbena prefers a **sunny** location. The soil should be **light, well drained** and **fertile**.

Tips
Lemon verbena is a half-hardy perennial that is best grown in a container in colder regions so it can be brought inside over the winter. It also works well in a formal herb or medicinal garden.

Recommended
A. triphylla produces narrow, pale green leaves that smell strongly of lemon. Tiny, white flowers tinged with pale purple emerge in early summer.

Features: aromatic foliage
Flower color: white tinged with pale purple **Height:** 3–4'
Spread: 18–36" **Hardiness:** half-hardy annual

Mint

Mentha

The cool, refreshing flavor of mint lends itself to tea and other hot or cold beverages. Mint sauce, made from freshly chopped mint leaves, is often served with lamb.

Growing

Mint grows well in **full sun** or **partial shade**. The soil should be **average to fertile, humus rich** and **moist**. These plants spread vigorously by rhizomes and will need a barrier in the soil to restrict their spread.

Tips

Mint is a good groundcover for damp spots. It grows well along ditches that may only be periodically wet. Mint also can be used in beds and borders but may overwhelm less vigorous plants.

The flowers attract bees, butterflies and other pollinators to the garden.

Recommended

There are many species, hybrids and cultivars of mint. Spearmint (**M. spicata**), peppermint (**M. x piperita**) and lemon mint (**M. x piperata** 'Citrata') are three of the most commonly grown culinary varieties. There are also more decorative varieties with variegated or curly leaves, as well as varieties with unusual, fruit-scented leaves.

Mint with lemon balm (above); *L. gracilis* 'Variegata' (below)

A few sprigs of fresh mint added to a pitcher of iced tea gives it an added zip.

Features: fragrant foliage; summer flowers **Flower color:** purple, pink, white **Height:** 6–36" **Spread:** 36" or more **Hardiness:** zones 4–8

Oregano·Marjoram
Origanum

O. vulgare 'Polyphont' (above); *O. vulgare* 'Polyphont' (below)

Oregano and marjoram are two of the best known and most frequently used herbs. They are popular in stuffings, soups and stews, and no pizza is complete until it has been sprinkled with fresh or dried oregano leaves.

Growing
Oregano and marjoram grow best in **full sun**. The soil should be of **poor to average fertility, neutral to alkaline** and **well drained**. The flowers attract pollinators to the garden.

Tips
These bushy perennials make a lovely addition to any border and can be trimmed to form low hedges.

Recommended
O. majorana (marjoram) is upright and shrubby with light green, hairy leaves. It bears white or pink flowers in summer and can be grown as an annual in areas where it is not hardy.

O. vulgare **var. hirtum** (oregano, Greek oregano) is the most flavorful culinary variety of oregano. This low, bushy plant has hairy, gray-green leaves and bears white flowers. Many other interesting varieties of *O. vulgare* are available, including plants with golden, variegated or curly leaves.

Features: fragrant foliage; summer flowers; bushy habit **Flower color:** white, pink **Height:** 12–32" **Spread:** 8–18" **Hardiness:** zones 5–8

Parsley
Petroselinum

P. crispum (above & below)

Although usually used as a garnish, parsley is rich in vitamins and minerals and is reputed to freshen the breath after garlic- or onion-rich foods are eaten.

Growing

Parsley grows well in **full sun** or **partial shade**. The soil should be of **average to rich fertility, humus rich, moist** and **well drained**. Direct sow seeds because the plants resent transplanting. If you start seeds early, use peat pots so the plants can be potted or planted out without disruption.

Tips

Parsley should be started where you mean to grow it. Containers of parsley can be kept close to the house for easy picking. The bright green leaves and compact growth habit make parsley a good edging plant for beds and borders.

Recommended

P. crispum forms a clump of bright green, divided leaves. This plant is biennial but is usually grown as an annual. Cultivars may have flat or curly leaves. Flat leaves are more flavorful; curly leaves are more decorative. Dwarf cultivars are also available.

Features: attractive foliage **Height:** 8–24"
Spread: 12–24" **Hardiness:** zones 5–8

Rosemary
Rosmarinus

R. officinalis (above & below)

To overwinter a container-grown plant, keep it in very light or partial shade in summer, and then put it in a sunny window indoors during the winter. Keep it well watered, but not soaking wet.

Rosemary's needle-like leaves are used to flavor a wide variety of foods, including chicken, pork, lamb, rice, tomato, potato and egg dishes.

Growing

Rosemary prefers **full sun** but tolerates partial shade. The soil should be of **poor to average fertility** and **well drained**. Place it in an area with good air circulation to prevent mildew.

Tips

In climates where rosemary is hardy, plant it in a shrub border. In colder regions, grow rosemary in a container as a specimen or with other plants. Include low-growing, spreading varieties in a rock garden or along the top of a retaining wall, or use them in hanging baskets and containers. Rosemary can also be trained into standard forms and trimmed to form topiary shapes.

Recommended

R. officinalis is a dense, bushy, tender evergreen shrub with narrow, dark green leaves. The habit varies somewhat between cultivars from upright to prostrate and spreading. Flowers usually come in shades of blue, but pink- or white-flowered cultivars are available. A cultivar called **'Arp'** can survive in zone 6 in a sheltered location with winter protection. Plants rarely reach their mature size when grown in containers.

Features: fragrant, evergreen foliage; summer flowers **Flower color:** usually bright blue, sometimes pink or white **Height:** 8"–4' **Spread:** 12"–4' **Hardiness:** zone 8

Thyme

Thymus

Thyme is a popular culinary herb used in soups, stews, casseroles and with roasts.

Growing

Thyme prefers **full sun**. The soil should be **neutral to alkaline** and of **poor to average fertility**. **Good drainage** is essential. It is beneficial to work leaf mold and sharp gravel into the soil to improve structure and drainage.

Tips

Thyme is useful for sunny, dry locations at the front of borders, between or beside paving stones, on rock gardens and rock walls, and in containers.

Once the plants have finished flowering, shear them back by about half to encourage new growth and to prevent the plants from becoming too woody.

Recommended

T.* x *citriodorus (lemon-scented thyme) forms a mound of lemon-scented, dark green foliage. The flowers are pale pink. Cultivars with silver- or gold-margined leaves are available.

T. vulgaris (common thyme) forms a bushy mound of dark green leaves. The flowers may be purple, pink or white. Cultivars with variegated leaves are available.

These plants are bee magnets when blooming; thyme honey is pleasantly herbal and goes very well with biscuits.

T. vulgaris (above); *T.* x *citriodorus* 'Argenteus' (below)

Features: bushy habit; fragrant, decorative foliage; flowers **Flower color:** purple, pink, white **Height:** 8–16" **Spread:** 8–16" **Hardiness:** zones 4–8

Ajuga
Ajuga

A. reptans 'Chocolate Chip' (above); 'Caitlin's Giant' (below)

Often labeled as a rampant runner, ajuga grows best where it can roam freely without competition.

Growing

Ajugas develop the best leaf color in **partial or light shade** but tolerate full shade. The leaves may become scorched when exposed to too much sun. Any **well-drained** soil is suitable. Divide these vigorous plants any time during the growing season.

Remove any new growth or seedlings that don't show the hybrid leaf coloring.

Tips

Ajugas make excellent groundcovers for difficult sites, such as exposed slopes and dense shade. They also look attractive in shrub borders, where their dense growth prevents the spread of all but the most tenacious weeds.

Recommended

A. genevensis (Geneva bugleweed) is an upright, noninvasive species that bears blue, white or pink spring flowers.

A. pyramidalis 'Metallica Crispa' (upright bugleweed) is a very slow-growing plant with bronzy brown, crinkly foliage and violet-blue flowers.

A. reptans (common bugleweed) is low growing and quick spreading. Its many cultivars offer more colorful, often variegated, foliage than the species.

Also called: bugleweed **Features:** late-spring to early-summer flowers; colorful foliage **Flower color:** purple, blue, pink, white; grown for decorative foliage **Height:** 3–12" **Spread:** 6–36" **Hardiness:** zones 3–8

Artemisia

Artemisia

Most of the artemisias are valued for their silvery foliage rather than for their insignificant flowers. Silver is the ultimate blending color in the garden because it enhances every hue combined with it.

Growing

Artemisias grow best in **full sun**. The soil should be of **low to average fertility** and **well drained**. These plants dislike wet, humid conditions.

Tips

Use artemisias in border plantings. Smaller species and dwarf cultivars can be included in rock gardens. The silvery gray foliage of artemisias makes them good backdrop plants for brightly colored flowers. They are also useful for filling in spaces between other plants.

Recommended

A. ludoviciana (white sage, silver sage) is an upright, clump-forming plant with silvery white foliage. The species is not grown as often as its cultivars, such as **'Silver King'** and **'Valerie Finnis.'** (Zones 4–8)

A. schmidtiana (silvermound artemisia) is a low, dense, mound-forming perennial with feathery, hairy, silvery gray foliage. **'Nana'** (dwarf silvermound) is very compact and grows only half the size of the species.

A. stelleriana **'Silver Brocade'** is a low-growing, creeping perennial that is sometimes mistaken for the annual

A. stelleriana 'Silver Brocade' (above)
A. ludoviciana 'Valerie Finnis' (below)

dusty miller. Soft, silver foliage covers the woody base. Tall, white stems appear in mid- to late summer supporting insignificant yellow flowerheads high above the fancy foliage. (Zones 2–8)

Use artemisia foliage for fresh or dried flower arrangements and wreaths.

Also called: wormwood, sage, white sage
Features: silvery gray, feathery or deeply lobed foliage **Flower color:** grown for foliage
Height: 6–36" **Spread:** 12–36" **Hardiness:** zones 3–8

Bluebunch Wheatgrass
Pseudoroegneria

P. spicata

This grass has gone through a number of botanical name changes over the years, but your local garden center experts are sure to help you to find this valuable native beauty in your city or town.

*T*his tall, cool season grass is not only beautiful throughout the summer months but is equally as nice poking through snow drifts in a winter landscape.

Growing
Bluebunch wheatgrass prefers **full sun** but tolerates partial shade. The soil should be **well drained**. Bluebunch wheatgrass cannot tolerate areas with high water tables or excessive moisture, but it thrives in dry and hot locations.

Tips
This ornamental grass is ideal for naturalized areas, xeriscaping or a 'no-water' garden and south-facing slopes. It works well in mixed borders as a tall, background element. This versatile native grass is great for those difficult areas with dry, poor soil where little else thrives.

If you refrain from cutting back bluebunch wheatgrass in fall, you'll be rewarded with a fine display throughout the winter months.

Recommended
P. spicata (*Agropyron inerme; Agropyron spicata;* beardless bluebunch wheatgrass) forms a clump of tall, medium-textured, green blades, and slender but stiff stems, topped with decorative flowering seedheads.

Features: tall, blade-like leaves and seedheads **Height:** 12–24" **Spread:** 10–12" **Hardiness:** zones 4–8

Hens and Chicks

Sempervivum

The genus name *Sempervivum* means 'always living,' which is appropriate for these fascinating and constantly regenerating plants.

Growing

Grow hens and chicks in **full sun** or **partial shade**. The soil should be of **poor to average fertility** and **very well drained**. Add fine gravel or grit to the soil to provide adequate drainage. Once the plant blooms, it dies. When you deadhead the faded flower, pull up the soft parent plant as well to provide space for the new daughter rosettes that sprout up, seemingly by magic. Divide by removing these new rosettes and rooting them.

Tips

These plants make excellent additions to rock gardens and rock walls, where they will even grow right on the rocks.

Recommended

S. tectorum is one of the most commonly grown hens and chicks. It forms a low-growing mat of fleshy leaved rosettes, each about 6–10" across. Small new rosettes are quickly produced, and they grow and multiply to fill almost any space. Flowers may be produced in summer but are not as common in colder climates. The flowers emerge in the summer months in shades of red, yellow, white and purple.

S. tectorum (above)

The little plantlets are simple to pass along. Just separate a 'chick' and you have the start of a whole colony of plants.

Features: succulent foliage; unusual flowers
Flower color: red, yellow, white, purple
Height: 3–6" **Spread:** 12" to indefinite
Hardiness: zones 3–8

Hosta
Hosta

H. 'Francee'

preferable to afternoon sun in partial shade situations. The soil should ideally be **fertile, moist** and **well drained**, but most soils are tolerated. Hostas are fairly drought tolerant, especially if given a mulch to help retain moisture.

Division is not required but can be done every few years in spring or summer to propagate new plants.

Breeders are always looking for new variations in hosta foliage. Swirls, stripes, puckers and ribs enhance the leaves' various sizes, shapes and colours. Sun-loving hostas have recently become the new rage for gardens.

Growing
Hostas prefer **light or partial shade** but will grow in full shade. Morning sun is

Slugs can cause unsightly damage to the beautiful foliage. If they are a problem, select 'slug resistant' varieties with thick and waxy leaves that are difficult for these creatures to feed upon.

Tips
Hostas make wonderful woodland plants and look very attractive when combined with ferns and other fine-textured plants. Hostas are also good plants for a mixed border, particularly when used to hide the ugly, leggy lower stems and branches of some shrubs. Hostas' dense growth and thick, shade-providing leaves allow them to suppress weeds.

Recommended
Hostas have been subjected to a great deal of crossbreeding and hybridizing, resulting in hundreds of cultivars. Visit your local garden center or get a mail-order catalog to find out what's available.

Also called: plantain lily **Features:** decorative foliage; summer and fall flowers **Flower color:** white or purple plants grown mainly for foliage **Height:** 4–36" **Spread:** 6"–6' **Hardiness:** zones 2–8

Indian Ricegrass
Achnatherum

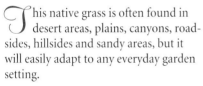

A. hymenoides (both photos)

This native grass is often found in desert areas, plains, canyons, roadsides, hillsides and sandy areas, but it will easily adapt to any everyday garden setting.

Growing

Indian ricegrass will grow in any **moderately fertile**, **moisture retentive**, **coarse**, **well-drained** soil in **full sun**. It easily adapts to a wide variety of soils but does not do well in wet or poorly drained soils. It can be propagated by both division or seed sow in spring.

Tips

This ornamental grass is highly drought tolerant and is graceful in form. It makes an excellent addition to a wildflower meadow and makes a good specimen plant.

Recommended

A. hymenoides (*Oryzopsis hymeniodes*) is a cool-season, densely clumped bunchgrass with needle-like leaves and loose clusters of flowers, resulting in decorative seedheads. Flowers are produced from May to July.

Also called: Indian millet, Indian mountain-rice grass, silky mountain rice **Features:** form; decorative seedheads **Height:** 1–2' **Spread:** 1–1¹/₂' **Hardiness:** zones 5–8

Indian ricegrass is native to sandy prairies and rocky slopes. The seeds were ground, mixed with water and cooked into a mush by Native Americans in Montana.

Little Bluestem
Schizachyrium

S. scoparium

Little bluestem offers year-round interest. This ornamental grass has graceful, swaying blades in spring and summer, followed by tall flower spikes in summer that evolve into fluffy plumes of seedheads that catch the light. Bronze and orange-toned foliage persists through the drifts of snow in winter, only to begin again in spring.

Growing

Little bluestem requires **full sun** and is tolerant of almost any soil type, except soil with inadequate drainage. It is known to seed itself readily. Propagate by both seed and division.

Tips

Little bluestem is a welcome addition to xeriscape gardens and naturalized areas. It also works well in mixed borders and in more contemporary settings.

The fluffy plumes are ideal for both fresh and dried floral arrangements.

Recommended

S. scoparium is a clump-forming grass. It produces light green, narrow blades 12–16" in length that become darker with maturity. The blade-like leaves are of a medium texture, somewhat hairy and soft to the touch. Flower spikes emerge through the foliage, supported by stems that rise high above the leaves. Decorative, fluffy plumes of ripening seedheads range in color from bronze to bright orange. **'Blaze'** is similar in form but displays more intense fall color, from reddish purples to orangy pinks.

Little bluestem is tolerant to drought but benefits from a little summer watering in more arid regions.

Also called: prairie beard grass, broom sedge **Features:** form; habit; decorative foliage and seedheads; winter interest **Height:** 2–4' **Spread:** 12–36" **Hardiness:** zones 3–8

Periwinkle

Vinca

Periwinkle is commonly known as an evergreen groundcover plant, but it's far more than that. Its reliability is second to none and its ease of growth is sure to please.

Growing

Grow periwinkle in **partial to full shade**. It will grow in any type of soil as long as it is not too dry. The plants will turn yellow if the soil is too dry or the sun too hot. Divide periwinkle in early spring or mid- to late fall, or whenever it is becoming overgrown. One plant can cover almost any size of area.

Tips

Periwinkle is a useful and attractive groundcover in a shrub border, under trees or on a shady bank, and it prevents soil erosion. Periwinkle is shallow-rooted and able to out-compete weeds, but it won't interfere with deeper-rooted shrubs.

If periwinkle begins to outgrow its space, it may be sheared back hard in early spring. The sheared-off ends may have rooted along the stems. These rooted cuttings may be potted up and given away as gifts, or may be introduced to new areas of the garden.

Recommended

V. minor (lesser periwinkle) forms a low, loose mat of trailing stems. Purple or blue flowers are borne in a flush in spring and sporadically all summer. **'Alba'** bears white flowers. **'Atropurpurea'** bears reddish purple flowers.

Features: trailing foliage; mid-spring to fall flowers **Flower color:** bluish purple, reddish purple, white **Height:** 4–8" **Spread:** indefinite **Hardiness:** zones 4–8

Sheep Fescue
Festuca

F. glauca 'Elijah Blue' (above); F. glauca (below)

Sheep fescue is relatively common throughout the prairies, as it was one of the first ornamental grasses to appear on the market over a decade ago. It has thrived in harsh conditions and continues to display its finest features.

Fescue specimens can be divided and replanted approximately every two or three years, or when they begin to die out in the centers. This will help to maintain their foliar color.

Growing

Sheep fescue prefers a location in **full sun** in **poor to moderately fertile** soil that is **well drained** and a little on the **dry** side.

Tips

Sheep fescue is valued for its low-growing tufts of foliage. It is frequently used in xeriscape settings, contemporary gardens and naturalized areas. Low-growing fescue also works well in rock and alpine gardens.

Recommended

F. glauca produces steely blue tufts of fine, needle-like blades of grass. Most varieties produce tan-colored spikes that emerge from mounds of blue grass, revealing small, tan flower plumes. A great many cultivars and hybrids are available.

Also called: fescue **Features:** foliar color and form; tan flower spikes; growth habit **Height:** 6–18" **Spread:** 10–12" **Hardiness:** zones 3–8

Snow-on-the-Mountain

Euphorbia

E. marginata with canna lily (above); *E. marginata* (below)

These mounding plants are admired for the bright white bracts that surround their tiny flowers. A second show of color appears in fall when the leaves turn purple, red or orange.

Growing

Snow-on-the-mountain grows well in **full sun** or **light shade**, in **moist, well-drained, humus-rich** soil of **average fertility**. These plants are drought tolerant and can be invasive in fertile soil. They do not tolerate wet conditions. Plant them in spring or fall.

Propagate snow-on-the-mountain with stem cuttings. Dip the cut ends in hot water to stop the sticky white sap from running.

Division is rarely required. These plants dislike being disturbed once established.

Tips

Use snow-on-the-mountain in a mixed or herbaceous border, rock garden or lightly shaded woodland garden.

Recommended

E. marginata is a vigorous growing, bushy plant with bright green, oval leaves with clear white margins. Petal-like white bracts surround tiny clusters of flowers in summer.

Also called: ghostweed **Features:** colorful bracts; low maintenance **Flower color:** white, greenish yellow **Height:** 24" **Spread:** 12" **Hardiness:** zones 4–8

Sweet Woodruff

Galium

Sweet woodruff is a groundcover that abounds with good qualities, including attractive light green foliage that smells like new-mown hay, abundant white, spring flowers and the ability to fill in garden spaces without taking over.

The dried leaves of sweet woodruff were once used to scent bed linens and freshen stale rooms.

Growing

This plant prefers **partial shade**. It will grow well, but will not bloom well, in full shade. The soil should be **humus rich** and **evenly moist**.

Tips

Sweet woodruff forms a beautiful green carpet and is a perfect woodland groundcover. Shear it back after it blooms to encourage growth of foliage that will crowd out weeds.

Recommended

G. odoratum is a low, spreading groundcover. Clusters of white, star-shaped flowers are borne in a flush in late spring and appear sporadically through mid-summer.

Features: perennial groundcover; late-spring to mid-summer flowers; fragrant foliage; habit
Flower color: white **Height:** 12–18"
Spread: indefinite **Hardiness:** zones 3–8

Glossary

Acid soil: soil with a pH lower than 7.0

Annual: a plant that germinates, flowers, sets seed and dies in one growing season

Alkaline soil: soil with a pH higher than 7.0

Basal leaves: leaves that form from the crown, at the base of the plant

Bract: a modified leaf at the base of a flower or flower cluster

Corm: a bulb-like, food-storing, underground stem, resembling a bulb without scales

Crown: the part of the plant at or just below soil level where the shoots join the roots

Cultivar: a cultivated plant variety with one or more distinct differences from the species, e.g., in flower color or disease resistance

Damping off: fungal disease causing seedlings to rot at soil level and topple over

Deadhead: to remove spent flowers to maintain a neat appearance and encourage a longer blooming season

Direct sow: to sow seeds directly in the garden

Dormancy: a period of plant inactivity, usually during winter or unfavorable conditions

Double flower: a flower with an unusually large number of petals

Genus: a category of biological classification between the species and family levels; the first word in a scientific name indicates the genus

Grafting: a type of propagation in which a stem or bud of one plant is joined onto the rootstock of another plant of a closely related species

Hardy: capable of surviving unfavorable conditions, such as cold weather or frost, without protection

Hip: the fruit of a rose, containing the seeds

Humus: decomposed or decomposing organic material in the soil

Hybrid: a plant resulting from natural or human-induced cross-breeding between varieties, species or genera

Inflorescence: a flower cluster

Male clone: a plant that may or may not produce pollen but that will not produce fruit, seed or seedpods

Neutral soil: soil with a pH of 7.0

Perennial: a plant that takes three or more years to complete its life cycle

pH: a measure of acidity or alkalinity; the soil pH influences availability of nutrients for plants

Rhizome: a root-like, food-storing stem that grows horizontally at or just below soil level, from which new shoots may emerge

Rootball: the root mass and surrounding soil of a plant

Seedhead: dried, inedible fruit that contains seeds; the fruiting stage of the inflorescence

Self-seeding: reproducing by means of seeds without human assistance, so that new plants constantly replace those that die

Semi-double flower: a flower with petals in two or three rings

Single flower: a flower with a single ring of typically four or five petals

Species: the fundamental unit of biological classification; the entity from which cultivars and varieties are derived

Standard: a shrub or small tree grown with an erect main stem, accomplished either through pruning and training or by grafting the plant onto a tall, straight stock

Sucker: a shoot that comes up from the root, often some distance from the plant; it can be separated to form a new plant once it develops its own roots

Tender: incapable of surviving the climatic conditions of a given region and requiring protection from frost or cold

Tuber: the thick section of a rhizome bearing nodes and buds

Variegation: foliage that has more than one color, often patched or striped or bearing leaf margins of a different color

Variety: a naturally occurring variant of a species

Index

Entries in **bold** type indicate the main plant headings.

Author Biographies

Dr. Bob Gough, Interim Associate Dean of Academic Programs at Montana State University's College of Agriculture, professor of horticulture and extension horticulture specialist, has published a dozen books on gardening. A nationally popular speaker and garden writer, his columns have appeared in Montana newspapers for a decade. He has published more than 40 research articles in horticultural journals and hundreds of popular articles in publications such as *Montana Magazine, Fine Gardening, National Gardening, Harrowsmith* and *Country Journal*. His long-running radio program, *Dr. Bob's Northern Gardening Tips*, is heard over more than a dozen stations in Montana, Wyoming and South Dakota, and his television show by the same name is broadcast over Montana's NBC affiliate stations.

Cheryl Moore-Gough has been a Montana gardener for more than 20 years. She holds a master's degree in horticulture from Montana State University, where she is an adjunct instructor in horticulture. Cheryl formerly served as a plant disease diagnostician in Montana State University's Schutter Diagnostic Laboratory, has instructed and supervised the Montana Master Gardener certification program, and has published in *Montana Magazine*.

Laura Peters is a certified Master Gardener with 15 gardening books to her credit. She has gained valuable experience in every aspect of the horticultural industry in a career that has spanned more than 16 years. She enjoys sharing her practical knowledge of organic gardening, plant varieties and gardening products with fellow gardeners.

Acknowledgments

We thank Kristin Petersen for her photography and Mark Majerus and Joseph D. Scianna (USDA NRCS Plant Materials Program, Bridger, MT) for use of their file photos. We also thank, finally, the gardeners of Montana who, by their numerous inquiries, fostered in us the certain knowledge that this book is needed.—*Dr. Bob Gough & Cheryl Moore-Gough*

A big thanks to my family and friends for their endless encouragement and support all these years. I would also like to thank the stellar team of Dr. Bob and Cheryl. Without their expertise and assistance, this book would have lacked that Montana touch. A special thank you to all those who allowed me to photograph their lovely gardens; to those, including Bluestem Nursery, who graciously answered all of my questions; and finally to those who kindly offered their beautiful images, including Michelle Meyer from Bailey Nurseries and Jan Hjalmarsson of Montana Plant Life (http://montana.plant-life.org).—*Laura Peters*